From Mrs Ross
With every [*barcode: D1588909*] the
coming yea

£1

Memories and Musings

By the Same Author

SPICY BREEZES FROM SUNNY CEYLON
(D. Wyllie & Son, Aberdeen)

THE BOOK OF OLD CASTLEHILL
(T. & A. Constable Ltd., Edinburgh)

Verse—

MUSINGS FROM MALTA
(*Galloway Gazette*, Newton Stewart)

Printed by THE DARIEN PRESS LTD., *Edinburgh.*

[*Photo by Lafayette.*

C. V. A. MACECHERN

Memories and Musings

C. V. A. MACECHERN

THE MORAY PRESS
EDINBURGH & LONDON
1954

To

WILLIE DEY FYFE,

The best of comrades

in College Rooms and on the Field.

" I remember the days of old."

CONTENTS

ILLUSTRATIONS

FOREWORD

By The Rt. Hon. Sir DAVID MAXWELL FYFE,
G.C.V.O., Q.C., M.P.

IN writing this foreword I feel that I am acting as deputy for my brother, to whom this book is dedicated. I know how much this dedication would have pleased him, and it is fitting that one of his relatives should acknowledge not only the honour of the dedication but the friendship which still flourishes twenty-eight years after his death.

For my first memories of the author I must hurry back through time for forty-five years, when my brother was a divinity student at King's College, Aberdeen, and I had attained the mature age of eight. I hope that no one will misunderstand me when I say that although I can remember how impressed I was at hearing for the first time the author and my brother preach, my keenest recollection is of the lighter side of their undergraduate life. I remember most clearly exerting arts of advocacy unsurpassed in my days at the Bar, when I as a small boy besought my mother to let me stay up another half-hour to hear the author sing another song, and if possible the duet with my brother which finished their programme for the night. Moreover, as reflected in admiring fraternal words, the author was a soccer player of almost legendary skill not only in representing his University but the First League Football Club of Aberdeen.

So much for my little corner of his past, the wide horizon of which is spread before us in this book. We feel, as only a true Highlander can make us feel,

> " the breezes blowing
> Fresh along the mountain side "

of his Highland boyhood. There rise again in the mirror of the mind, which is so much more comforting than the mirror of everyday life, not only the sun shining on the granite of Aberdeen, but the old town that nestles round the crown of King's College and Old Machar.

Like all good Scots, our author has added to his love for his native land by absence in far places and has given us unforgettable pictures of Malta and Ceylon. For at least five hundred years the Scot Abroad has been an essential part of our national community. Our robust belief in the benefit he conferred in foreign parts is true in our author's case.

Ultimately, however, the reader will value the book for its living and kindly picture of twentieth-century Scotland and Scots. This book breathes the spirit of the great words of Neil Munro with regard to the Highlands :—

> " . . . praise God for His favour
> That ane sae unworthy should heir sic estate."

That spirit honours not only our country but the man who breathes it after a long and active life in the service of Scotland and her Church.

THE HAPPINESS OF A HIGHLAND MANSE

" The smiles and tears
Of boyhood's years."

—MOORE.

ONE of the summer visitors to the home of my childhood was a very vivacious lady from Middlesex. She resolved, after that visit, that she would marry no one but a Scottish minister. With that object in view she returned to Scotland in the following year, and in her eager hunt she left no stone unturned. Eventually in that same manse she met her fate. Discovering that the young minister was an ardent lover of Robert Burns, she proceeded to learn some of the poet's songs and to study something of his life and fortunes.

" I love your poet Burns," she said with rapture. " I adore his lyrics, but my favourite is the one about the manse."

" And which one is that ? " asked the minister.

" Oh, the one with the chorus ' A MANSE A MANSE FOR A' THAT.' "

A popular song earlier in the century was " There's Something about a Sailor." So, also, there is something about a manse ; and if I were to be given my choice, I think I would still choose to enter upon the adventure of life within the sanctity of a Scottish manse. Behind it there is a rich tradition ; its sons and daughters have furnished a large place in the book of Scottish biography ; and within it " plain living and high thinking " has been the order of the day. Robert Burns in his immortal poem " The Cottar's Saturday Night " has depicted the cottage homes of Caledonia, with the father turning over the big ha' Bible at the family worship ; and such a picture was found also in the old Scottish manses. My earliest recollection is of our own family worship—each member of the household with an open Bible, from which

1

was read a verse in turn. Sometimes we sang a hymn or a psalm and, as we knelt, father gave thanks to God for the mercies of another day and commended all present and our absent friends to the kindly protection of the Father of all.

Still vivid in my memory is the setting forth for the annual summer holiday, spent at our maternal grandmother's in Moulin, under the shadow of the majestic Ben Vrackie. The luggage was piled up at the front door, the gas was turned off at the meter, the blinds were drawn and already the cab was waiting without. But not yet could the key be turned in the lock; first the family must assemble in the dining-room and engage in the morning prayer. And we felt then, and we feel to-day, that our holiday was all the more beneficial and blessed because father had invoked on our behalf God's blessing upon the month's relaxation to which we were excitedly looking forward.

Budgeting in the manse for a large family, with three of the boys already at the University, on a small stipend, required a touch of careful genius. How it was managed remains part of the mystery of things to myself; for, in addition to ourselves, the manse welcomed a succession of guests, ministers and others, among whom were young students from farther north and west. Some of these, I know, remember to this day with a genuine gratitude the friendship and the guidance which were given them amidst their first loneliness away from their Highland homes.

Recently I revisited my native town of Inverness. How small appeared to be the garden where once we played at hide-and-seek; where first we engaged in a game of football and where, under the chestnut tree, we enjoyed the earliest romance of youth. A picnic to the outskirts of the town was a day's adventure. At Christmas time there was the certainty of skating on the frozen pond at Loch-na-Sanais, so picturesquely situated. Saturday was marked by the issue of pocket money—and threepence went a long way! But our greatest recklessness was when we were given sixpence to admit us to a Saturday evening concert. These were held in the

Music Hall and drew crowded audiences. The talent was for the most part local; but on occasions a " star " was brought from Aberdeen, among them being David Thomson from the Seaside Pavilion and Violet Davidson, who was later to become his wife. Many of the artistes and items are easily remembered. There was the famous trio Christie, Ballantyne and Munro, and Kate Fraser with her rich contralto voice. How many a time we heard Alick Sinclair sing " Where are the Boys of the Old Brigade ? " never without his favourite mannerism—the playing with the large fob dangling from his silver watch-chain. Father believed in the cultural value of good music, and because of it as boys we had the privilege of hearing Paderewski and Clara Butt on the occasion of their first visit to the Highland capital. But even more to our liking was the starring visit of Funny Frame with his whimsical nonsensicalities. The greatest thrill, however, in our later boyhood was the showing of Calder's Cinematograph with its accompanying concert party. Already we had been introduced to the Phonograph; but the Cinema was something even more wonderful. The showing of each film was of short duration and imposed a considerable strain upon our eyes; for the figures as they moved across the screen appeared to be stricken with St Vitus' Dance, and the impression was that torrential rain was coming down upon the scene depicted, even when it happened to be the interior of a royal palace. Inverness had a share in the pioneering work of the movies, for it was, I think, Mr MacKenzie, watchmaker, of the fancy goods shop in Inglis Street, who was the first to " shoot " a picture in the North, one of his very earliest being the Inverness Volunteers marching out from the Drill Hall *en route* for the sham fight at Dunain.

Other days which stand out in my memory include the occasion of the transference of the old Royal Academy to the new buildings on the Crown, when we marched as children, a few of us waving flags, feeling that we were making history. To-day, where the former seat of learning stood there is a steam bakery. The " plain living and high thinking " have given place to plain thinking and high living ! But now from the distance I salute the teachers who suffered under me more than I suffered under them : Grace Middleton, who first taught me that reading was an art ; and later giants such as Mr Cockburn and Mr Reid ; M. Delevault, the Art Master, whose artistic aid put the finishing touches to the stage at our annual School Concert ; and W. S. Roddie of beloved memory, whose contribution to the musical culture of Inverness has left its mark to the third generation.

In the old Raining's School I remember best of all Alick Martin who, like Burns at the plough, had " no rival " in his wielding of the strap or the cane ; and Dr Alexander McBain, the Headmaster, whose scholarship we as boys were too young to appreciate fully. In the High School, under the Rectorship of Mr Wallace, we continued our studies and enjoyed on occasions the coveted privilege of ringing the great bell in the tower. More attention was given to religious instruction than is the case in the overcrowded curriculum to-day ; and when the MacDougall Trust examination was held in the spring we could have narrated the travels of the apostle Paul with a greater correctness of detail than he could have recapitulated them himself. Trotter, Barclay and Low, McConnachie, Lowson and Kennedy were all among our teachers, and Agnes Dobbie, whose long and faithful record entitled her to retire with honour. In my scrapbook I retain a photograph of standard VI, and it may not be without significance that Mr Kennedy, at that time at the very outset of his distinguished career, is standing right behind myself with his hand resting upon my shoulder !

Twenty-five years after I had left the Inverness Academy I was invited as one of the guests of the evening at the Old Boys' Dinner and proud I was to accept. In the course of my reply to the toast I gave a vivid but much exaggerated representation of my old Headmaster, the scholarly Dr Watson, laying about me with his four-fingered strap. At the conclusion of the dinner an attractive-looking young man in immaculate dinner dress came up and said to me, " Thank you very much, Mr MacEchern, for that graphic picture of the Headmaster. It was my Dad to the very life ! " I was being addressed by one of the distinguished sons of an equally distinguished father.

Most of the teachers of my schooldays are dead and gone. It is too late now to make amends for the boyish pranks which we played upon them but which, doubtless, they enjoyed in spite of the annoyance which their dignity as Masters enforced them to display.

BABY LANGUAGE IS ONE OF THE MINOR CRIMES

> " *Zinkty, tinkty, my black hen,*
> *She lays eggs for gentlemen.*"
>
> —Old counting rhyme.

HAVING ears, we hear not. It is an age-long weakness of the human race. And yet perhaps it is well that it is so ; for there are many voices, but only a very few of these are worthy of our attentive ear. Among them, surely, is the voice of the professor—in his own sphere of profession. Among my cuttings I have a brief report of a professorial onslaught upon parents for a method of address to their young offspring for which, this professor declares, the parents ought to be thoroughly ashamed. His protest is against what he terms " baby language."

" I have no use for baby language," says the writer. " A grown-up ought to be ashamed of himself or herself who can descend to this sort of thing. It is up to you and me to be intelligent with our children." And this professor's advice to parents is : " Talk to your child intelligently."

In this matter of approach to children I am happy to find myself backed up by so eminent a teacher. When presented by the proud parents to their gurgling infantile offspring, I have always left it to the endearing mother to say to the child, " Weeny, weeny, teetums, teetums," and to the doting father to chirp, " Wonky, winky, woodles, diddums, doodums " ; but I myself invariably surprise the parents and delight the infant by asking such simple questions as, " Well, what do you think of this world ? " or " Have you any particular views on the present international situation ? " or even " What is your opinion of the Budget, my little son ? " It is astonishing how light will brighten up their little faces when they are addressed in this intelligent manner, and you can hear their gurgle of appreciation and gratitude.

What a wonderful world will open up for the child when the grown-ups discard the old " baby talk " and learn to respect the natural intelligence of their children. Doubtless the Church will give a lead in this connection. I can picture some minister visiting a home in his parish to find a parent walking the floor bearing in his arms an infant who should have been abed long since. " Wassums not wantums to bye-bye yettums ? " chants the parent. But the minister protests : " Look here. It is high time this infant was in bed. It is not what he wants, nor what you want, nor what anyone wants ; it is what I want. He ought to be in bed ; I move accordingly." And forthwith the child is removed, perfectly satisfied when he has been told that, by a majority, it has been decided that he should surrender himself into the soothing arms of Morpheus.

The child of the car conductor is quite as obstreperous as any other child ; but the car conductor, from sheer force of practice with his customers during the rush hour, talks intelligently to him when he arrives home, and the baby appreciates his grammatical speech and duly responds. For example, when his child has already eaten more than enough but still cries out for more, the father does not argue with him or indulge in coaxing nonsensicalities of meaningless language, which merely aggravates the hungry appetite. No, our conductor-parent simply announces to the overfed child, " Full up ! " and all is well.

If this baby language is wrong, so also are the baby songs which have held sway in the nursery. We have been told that musically we are a C 3 nation and ethically not much better than that. But why is it so ? Surely because of the idiotic nonsense which we sing into the astonished ears of our tender offspring. All that must end, and we must learn to sing to

[*Photo by MacMahon, Inverness.*

WHEN WE WERE VERY YOUNG

The author and his brother Fergus, from the old
Family Album.

[*To face page* 6.

the little children intelligently, approaching them in the spirit of Fitz Eustace—

> " Now must I venture, as I may,
> To sing his favourite rondelay."

Our children for many a long day have been brought up on nonsense rhymes ; and when their nursery songs did contain sense, the moral in too many cases was very questionable.

> " Little Tommy Tiddlemouse
> Lived in a little house ;
> He stole fishes
> From other men's ditches."

And then you wonder why the sheriff is always having to reprimand poachers ! Again, far too many of our nursery rhymes appeal to the stomach of the child and far too few to the receptive mind.

> " Pat-a-cake, pat-a-cake, baker's man,
> Bake me a cake as fast as you can.
> Prick it and dot it and mark it with B,
> And put it in the oven for baby and me."

The professor is right. " Talk to your children intelligently " and cease all this goo-goo baa-baa nonsense. What respect can a child have for a parent who dares to address him with " Giggily, giggily, googily gumpies " ? Take a lesson rather from the teacher of psychology, who may be heard seriously addressing his son in the cradle after this manner : " My boy, never forget the influence of the subconscious upon the conscious life. The subconscious, remember, harbours all the springs of all our obscurely-motivated passions, impulses, convictions, likes, dislikes and prejudices. Our intentions, hypotheses, fancies, persuasions, convictions and, in several, all our non-rational operations come from it." And we may not be surprised if the infant, fully appreciative, is heard to reply, " Gee, pop, you've sure spoken it ! "

JUVENILE ASPIRATIONS

My first literary effort to delight me by its appearance in print was a descriptive letter to *The Lady* under the pseudonym " Nevada." Encouraged by this initial success I aspired to the joke column of the *Weekly News*. Three entries in my diary will best present my success.

> " *October 17th.*—Sent in a joke to the *Weekly News*. There are prizes of 5s. and 2s. 6d.
> " *October 25th.*—Received a letter to-day with a P.O. 5s., having won first prize in the joke column.
> " *October 26th.*—Father very pleased with my success. Encourages me to go in for literature."

It was only on rereading my diary years later that it dawned upon me that father had been merely *pulling my leg*, although this phrase had not yet come into common use. That I took his approval of my effort seriously at the time is seen from a short article which I wrote and which appeared in the *People's Friend* a few weeks later.

Mr A. A. Milne, concerning a subject in which he is well versed, wrote this : " Everybody in England over the age of fifteen (20,000,000) earnestly desires to write a play, which play, when written, will be, in his or her opinion, a good play. Of the plays written ninety-nine per cent. will be bad plays— of a badness inconceivable." At the age of fifteen, being no exception, I was struck with the brave ambition to produce a magazine ; and produce it I did. Doubtless it came under the category of the ninety-nine per cent., but it afforded me a very great amount of pleasure and satisfaction and perhaps a little amusement to my small circle of subscribers. At the time I was living with an older brother who was then minister of his first parish—the Island of Coll ; and this magazine was part of his scheme of tuition, taking the place of the stereotyped essay among the English lessons. We hear much about the freedom of the press, but as producer of the *Coll*

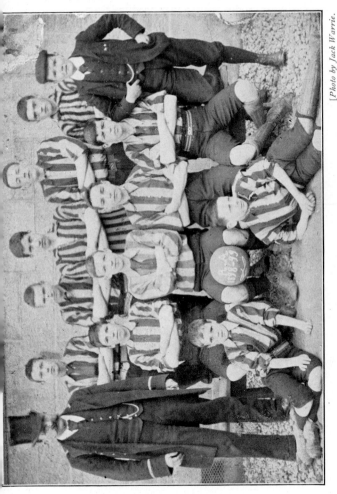

[*Photo by Jack Warrie.*

INVERNESS ROYAL ACADEMY FOOTBALL CLUB, 1898-99

Back row—W. Garrow, J. Stewart, F. MacKay, C. Macpherson, D. Forbes, C. MacIntosh.
Middle row—Mr Watson (Janitor), S. MacIntosh, P. Macdonald (Captain), MacIntosh, Finlayson.
In front—C. V. A. MacEchern and W. Duncan.

[*To face page* 8.

ABERDEEN UNIVERSITY FOOTBALL CLUB, 1907-8

Back row—I. S. Moir, John Clark, Esq., A. W. Ross, K. Ross, W. B. Thomson, F. J. S. Paterson,
D. W. Macleod, John MacHardy.

Front row—F. L. Stuart, C. S. Marr, J. R. Mackenzie, C. V. A. MacEchern (Captain), E. Simpson,

[*To face page* 9.

Warbler I enjoyed a licence which might have been the envy of every editor in Britain. I was my own censor, and some of my playful thrusts regarding some of the islanders must have come near to the borderline of libel. They certainly were made to see themselves as one other saw them, and I marvel now that they took it all with such kindly grace. One issue included such daring articles as " How to dodge the Gamekeeper," " The Day the old Dog died " (illustrated with a string of sausages in the butcher's window) and " Practical Jokes worth Trying." A copy of my little magazine was sent to the Editor of the *Highland News* in my native town, and to my infinite delight a week later I opened that journal to find that it contained a brief review of my publication. It is only when I reread it from the distance now that I fully appreciate the generous indulgence of the writer of the paragraph ; but you can imagine how greatly it pleased my boyish heart.

" The *Coll Warbler* which, we are assured, is a Christmas annual to amuse youngsters, is the production of our young friend Mr Victor MacEchern, who is the author, editor, illustrator, manager, printer and publisher of the *Warbler* all rolled in one. In an article entitled ' Behind the Scenes,' the editor gives a pathetic account of his many trials and tribulations in the field of journalism. He says : ' There was a round mahogany table on which I did my printing. I used a cyclostyle, which was a complete success. On the first occasion, however, as I was not acquainted with the instrument, the pages became hopelessly mixed up. The result was embarrassing ; for when the issue appeared, the article on one page did not coincide with what had gone before. For instance, after reading about the good qualities of Mrs So-and-So's baby, you continue the article on the following page and find that " it should be wrapped in a floured cloth and boiled for two hours and a quarter, when it is ready for the table ! " It is some seconds before you perceive that you are at the cookery notes, which have been continued from a previous page.' Altogether the work—which must have given the young author some trouble—is a meritorious one despite a few printers' errors."

2

SUNDAY

*" And that's the day that comes betwixt
A Saturday and Monday."*

—HENRY CAREY.

IN the old manse, as in many a home throughout the land, Christmas Day was the happiest in all the year. If it was touched with mystery for us children, Santa Claus—probably at the instigation of my mother, or it may have been father—always included in our stocking something which might be useful. Among other gifts there was certain to be a diary; and I have continued throughout my life to keep a diary and in later days a book also of cuttings. I would encourage all boys to do the same, for in after-years much pleasure and amusement is derived from a perusal of the diaries of other days. I do not mean the business type of diary which hangs upon the wall with a page for every week, so that visitors can see at a glance where you are dining on Friday and who is expected to call on Saturday; not the kind of diary which reminds you of the date for the renewal of your wireless licence and the day when your income tax is due. My diary is a much more private thing and has a full page for every day. It commands respect because of its very binding, and one learns to open and close it as a very sacred thing. The contents are very personal, but some items are of general interest.

On 21st December 1902 I recorded this in my diary :—

" Father preached a terrific sermon in church to-night."

Some of his sermons are still vivid in my mind. His evening service was usually attended by a large congregation; occasionally the church was full. There was at that time no instrumental music in St Mary's, but there was an eager choir, the conducting being under the leadership of Mr Simon Fraser who, with his long white beard, looked to us like one of the ancient patriarchs. Before commencing, a white cardboard was set up facing the congregation bearing the name of the tune. The key was struck with the aid of a tuning fork, or more often by means of a small instrument into which the precentor blew. My father, who had earlier published some booklets on church music, was proud of the congregational singing, but we ourselves sometimes thought that the number of verses might have been curtailed. The reading of the Scripture was interspersed with brief expository comments; as when, in reading of Mary at the grave, he looked up from the Book and said, " Poor body; her heart was sore."

It was customary at the outset of the service for the banns of marriage to be proclaimed, each intimation being made on three successive Sundays. The Christmas season was the popular time for marriages in the Highland capital, and on one occasion as many as sixty names were read out. There were one or two Sundays when the banns were publicly objected to by someone in the congregation. The objector was invited to the vestry, where a shilling had to be deposited and the objection considered. The forenoon service in St Mary's Parish Church was held at the canonical hour of 11—and in the Gaelic language; the evening worship, in English, was at 6.30. My father's sermon commenced about 7.15 and the 8 o'clock curfew in the town steeple invariably accompanied his peroration. His discourses were a fine blend of the evangel and topical illustrations. Fire and brimstone were reserved for special occasions, as when a lurid description of the great fire of Chicago, which he himself had witnessed, prepared the way for the delineation of a still greater fire reserved for not a few delinquents in the congregation !

But my father's most daring exaggeration, albeit quite unconsciously made, was on the Sunday succeeding the great international football match at Hampden Park, when he decided to deliver a sermon on the lost sense of values as evidenced by the increasing craze for sport. Hearing the boys excitedly discussing the match on the Saturday evening, when the *Football Times* provided a detailed description of the game, father elicited some information on the subject and carefully noted it on his manuscript. Twenty-two players; one hundred and five thousand spectators; gate drawings, £640.

[The figures are not authentic, but they will serve the occasion.]
On Sunday evening, to a full church, father launched out at
the top of his form. " At Glasgow, yesterday," he declared,
" there was a football match. How many engaged in the
game ? Twenty-two players. How many people crowded in
to see the match as spectators ? Six hundred and forty people.
And how much money did they spend on their ninety minutes'
enjoyment ? ONE HUNDRED AND FIVE THOUSAND POUNDS ! "
. . . At the manse supper table that night we challenged the
preacher and pointed out that according to his statement each
spectator must have paid about £200 for his ticket ! But
father was not in the least bit disconcerted, his immediate
comment being, " Well, after all, they are none the worse of
a little exaggeration ! " I am not aware that any lecturer on
Pastoral Theology has ever touched on this point in his dealing
with " the sermon."

SOME EXTRACTS FROM AN EARLY DIARY

SCHOOLBOY journals are all very much alike and a few extracts
from my own earliest diaries may remind you of the kind of
entries which you made in yours. The first refers to a short
period when we were without a housekeeper in the manse of
Coll and we boys had to tackle the cooking.

" *Monday*, 20*th*.—I am bewailing the day our housekeeper
left. The fire went out twice this morning and there was not
a dry stick to be had. Woe is me."

" *Wednesday*, 22*nd*.—I lit the kitchen fire to-day and it
went magnificently. The oven is very hot and I have half a
mind to cook something fancy."

A lengthy description of the culinary results of my efforts
follows and then is added : " I forgot to say that the meat—
stewed mutton cut off the flank—was a little burnt to-day at
dinner owing to the water in the pot running dry."

" *Saturday*, 25*th*.—I managed to cook a bread pudding
to-day and none of us are feeling well to-night."

"*Thursday*, 13*th*.—My free sample collection is not yet very large, as it only contains fruit pills, cocoas and eruption remedy."

"*Wednesday*, 9*th*.—I found two eggs in a nest beneath the pulpit in the church to-day."

"*Thursday*, 10*th*.—Neil Gilchrist clipped Hector's hair with the sheep shears. He did it wonderfully well."

"*Sunday*, 11*th*.—Last Sunday I got a present of Fergus's good jacket and waistcoat which were rather tight for him. They fit me pretty well."

The following extracts are from my diary at Inverness :—

"*Thursday*, 15*th*.—I saw General Buller at the station and helped to cheer him."

"*Wednesday*, 28*th*.—Johnnie gave me 3s. 6d. to-day for my birthday and I bought a 1s. 6d. albo silver chain in Medlock's."

"*Tuesday*, 17*th*.—Went to Sanger's Circus to-night and got a fine row when I arrived home for spending a shilling in entry money when half of it was intended for Fergus."

"*Saturday*, 28*th*.—Bought Fergus's watch for 3s. 6d. Borrowed that amount from Meg to pay for it."

"*Wednesday*, 13*th*.—Thirteenth is lucky. Father went to Creich to-day. I carried his bag along to the station, for which I received the handsome sum of 1s."

"*Tuesday*, 7*th*.—Mother bought me a pair of football boots to-day. Hurrah ! "

"*Saturday*, 22*nd*.—Fergus went to the Saturday Evening Concert to-night and saw the management. The result is that he is booked for next Saturday to sing two comic songs and two encores. His fee for a start is 7s. 6d., of which I have agreed to get 1s. for playing his accompaniments."

"*Friday*, 28*th*.—Practised with Fergus for to-morrow's concert."

"*Saturday*, 29*th*.—Fergus sang to-night at Saturday Evening Concert in Music Hall. It was the rowdiest audience I ever saw or heard. Orange peels and bags of various sweets, etc., were thrown, but Fergus escaped pretty whole. However, he got his fee, 7s. 6d."

"*Tuesday, 2nd.*—It was 8.30 when I awoke, swallowed my breakfast in a great hurry—might have choked—and bolted off to school."

"*Monday,* 15*th.*—Got some ipecacuanha wine from mother for my cough."

On the last page of the diary from which these extracts are taken there is a page on which are written *Things to Remember*.

"Don't forget to practice the mandoline."

"Pick up a pin when you see one."

"'Honesty is the best policy.' If you want another slice of cake, just say so frankly and you will get it, with something else gratis when the visitors have gone off."

"Don't thump the piano too hard, or people may think that your sister is playing."

"Don't keep letting the cat out of the bag."

Looking back over these old diaries of mine, I am glad that they were rescued from the spring cleaning bonfire to which so much was annually consigned. I hope that you also have kept yours.

> "When you are old and grey and full of sleep
> And nodding by the fire, take down this book,
> And slowly read—and dream."

THE CHRISTMAS PARTY IN THE ISLAND

"*Beloved, a Good New Year.*"

—D. MACECHERN.

IN my Hebridean Island of long ago there were joys and there were sorrows; but the sorrows are forgotten and we remember only the joys. During the long dark winter there were only occasional entertainments; yet the infrequency of these added to the relish of our enjoyment. There was no wireless; there were no travelling companies of entertainers; we had to provide our own enjoyments, and not the least of these was the Christmas Party at the manse. Have you forgotten that one night in the year ?

Sons of the Island, scattered in far distant places in the west or over in the orient where the sun never tires of shining and the trees are never bare of leaves, recall the old days and how the wintry atmosphere induced the Christmas mood. Surely the work on the farms was accomplished in record time that day, and lassies with nature's bloom on their cheeks and hefty lads, who had held their own against the Glasgow Fairites in the summer sports, made their way with the swinging step through the sands that led to the manse, under the stars. On Sunday they had been to the little church at Clabbach to hear again the story of the shepherds who were guided by a star to where the holy Child was born, and under the spell of my brother Dugald's sermon they had known the place as holy ground and for them the very Gate of Heaven. But to-night the manse windows are bright with light from within, the hall is decked with evergreens provided by the factor, whose kilted sons and charming daughters are among the young revellers. The hall lamp is hung with the mystic mistletoe, and the young folk will prove themselves pagan enough to observe the kissing rites to which the symbol overhead invites.

The early shyness of the evening was soon put to flight, and by the time the pudding stage was reached around the festive board every guest was tuned up to the highest pitch of merriment. The finding of the lucky charms was hailed with cheers, and who could have been more suitably the finder of the " ring " than Bella from Breachacha ? John Ferguson was disappointed to find in his portion of pudding nothing more than the " button " ; but he braved it out by remarking " Just what I was wanting ! " Decked in our variously coloured headgear from the crackers we entered the manse drawing-room, and the minister at the piano gave us some rousing songs of his college days. Then followed the old-fashioned games, when each youth paid with brave relish the forfeit of his failure in the game. What has become of the girl whose name we called up the chimney ? Where now are the flowers of the carpet? Once in a while in distant places of the earth we chance upon them and our faces glow in the midst of happy recollection. For the children of the Island are now widely scattered and the home circle is never now complete. No longer do we cover the road from the old manse with our chosen beloved, when high hopes were in our hearts as the Old Year gave place to the New.

> Home we went, you remember,
> At midnight on hill paths frozen,
> With Margaret the golden-haired,
> And lily-limbed, sweet-throated Morag.
> The Old Year dead, and each youth
> Kissing his maiden and saying,
> " Beloved ! a good New Year."

Was it not the minister himself who gave us that verse? But the days that were are now no more for ever. The old manse is derelict; and were I to return and make my way through the long grasses and nettles in the desolate overgrown garden and peer through the broken window from which at that early Christmas the gay light streamed, I should see now an empty grate and the ashes of long ago.

THE VILLAGE CONCERT

> " *Is there an ear to hear aright*
> *The voice that sings?* "

> —MURRAY.

LET me endeavour to portray here what must have been a familiar function to all who have lived in the country—the Village Concert. It was held in the school and the children scarcely recognised the place, for a platform had been erected and tastefully arranged with curtains from the manse drawing-room, handsome bowls of flowers from the Lodge and a highly coloured carpet from the schoolhouse. A variety of oil lamps, with reflectors improvised from the lids of old biscuit tins, served as footlights and made us feel that we were real artistes. The moon was at its full and such a night of stars was surely never seen even in the far Orient. Additional interest was added to the evening's gathering, for the old laird and his house party, including Stewart of Achnacone and Rider Haggard, were present. Had we not all read some of Haggard's books ? The latter had graciously consented to preside and, when the hall was at last crowded, his opening remarks were brief and to the point as he assured the audience of a capital evening ahead of them. The schoolmaster was all on edge, not because he was down for a violin solo but because the choir of children was responsible for the opening item. Arithmetic and geography had suffered during the week, since much of the school time had been devoted to rehearsing ; but the choir, in spite of the weakness of the juvenile male members, rose to the occasion in " Ye Mariners of England," followed by the encore " Let the Hills resound with Song." Bella and Jeannie Irvine delighted with a duet ; Walter Ross, the most juvenile of the performers, recited as boys of his tender age do, and there was an excusable stamping of the feet when Miss Flora Maclean from Arileod roused us to a high pitch of enthusiasm with her Highland selection on the piano. Variety was lent by the manse boys, who appeared in the role of nigger minstrels. The burnt cork was only partially removed when they were called for their second turn— Offenbach's " Blind Beggars," with the libretto of which they took marked liberties. The chairman greeted them with the announcement, " Ah, here they come—comparatively clean ! " A solo by the minister—" The Snowy Breasted Pearl "—was less of a novelty than it might have been, for was not his predecessor, the Rev. George Maclennan, also a vocalist ? Then came the schoolmaster himself, a real disciplinarian ; so that even when his fiddle broke into a Highland Strathspey the juvenile section of the audience restrained the urge to mark time with their feet. It is good to know that his children have inherited their father's musical gifts and that James MacTaggart, the youngest, is now a distinguished

church organist and teacher of music on the edge of Glasgow.
The programme would not have been complete without the
bagpipes; and Calum Kennedy and Johnnie MacFadyen
gave of their best—the music which we had been hearing
from the manse as they practised at Benmeanach and Bally-
hough for weeks before the concert. But the concert comes
to an end; the customary votes of thanks to chairman and
performers have been given with heartiness; and then the
homeward trek. Full five miles of rough road we footed it;
but what was distance when the heart was young and youth
and beauty stepped out in unison?

Those were the days and the events which inspired the
minister's muse. It was then that he wrote:—

> " O for the sound of the surf
>   On the edge of the world,
> And the cot, with its thatch of turf,
>   On the edge of the world;
> And the barefooted maiden I knew,
>   And the hearts that were simple and true,
> Where our wants and our sorrows were few,
>   On the edge of the world."

From the other edge of the world sons and daughters of
my Hebridean Island recall those days " when earth was
nigher heaven than now "; in far Saskatoon the music of
some emigrant piper stirs the hearts of assembled kinsfolk;
and in Massachusetts the singer of a long-forgotten song
kindles old memories of the past. Some, prospering under
Eastern skies, would fain transport themselves for a season
to hear again the music of the Atlantic waves breaking on the
northern shores. Let others return in thought

> " To the glory that was Greece
>   And the grandeur that was Rome ";

we are content to remember the goodness that was ours
in the golden days of youth, in " the morning of the world "
for us.

THE SUNNIEST SEASON OF LIFE

" *Not hate, but glory, made these chiefs contend,*
And each brave foe was in his soul a friend."

—POPE.

A VISIT to the classic playing-fields at King's College, Aberdeen, always affords me a strange pleasure and at once a host of phantom figures make their appearance. Among them are the bearers of such names as Stanley Glass, H. R. Finlayson, Shand, A. G. Ellis, H. G. M. Wilson, W. D. Fyfe and the brothers Twort. Outstanding among the rugger players were Middleton, Buchart, Tocher, Findlay, Milne, George Cheyne and R. S. Clark. But my happiest and clearest recollections are of the soccer club. Arthur Murray and his colleagues had already graduated, although I was to receive his close attention later in games against the Queen's Park, of which he was the brilliant centre-half. In my Bajan year Jock Sangster was the popular captain of the University team, his long lanky legs operating in a tackle a fraction of a second sooner than his opponent expected ; and among my earliest companions on the field were David Mackenzie, David Gourlay, big Jock MacHardy, little McQuhat and Jimmy Macdonald from my own town of Inverness—a nursery of footballers. But our most attractive all-round sportsman was Kenneth Ross, already a triple " Blue," as he was to become later a triple graduate.

Athletic groups now hanging on my study walls help to keep those football days fresh in my memory. There are goalkeepers such as the dignified Bob Clark. How he loathed a threat of snow when taking the field ; and yet, was he not destined to accompany Shackleton to the Antarctic ? F. J. S. Paterson and Baillie Thomson were others who stood between the uprights. In the full-back division we had defenders like E. A. Pearson, Bremner and A. W. Ross. Our strongest half-back three were Bill Smith, a pioneer in the art of positioning ; David Macleod, a real iron stanchion ; and Jimmy

(Puddin') Gordon, whose feeding of his forwards was cool and correct. In the forward position there was keen competition for placings. Among right wingers we had Alex. (Buckie) Smith, Ernest Simpson and J. R. Mackenzie. Artistes on the left wing included Colin Munro, almost as tricky and aggravating as the great Bert ("Plout") Murray himself; J. R. Park and C. S. Marr, with Duggie Bruce from the manse of Banff as our dashing pivot. Frankie Stuart was our most versatile reserve. I was proud to captain the team in the season 1907-08.

My first away game was at Stonehaven: we were defeated. On the following Saturday the second eleven travelled to the same ground and defeated our vanquishers by a margin of two goals; and on the next Wednesday in *Alma Mater* there appeared a caustic letter to the Editor from someone in the Logic class suggesting that the logical conclusion was that, in the forthcoming Inter-varsity encounter, the second eleven should do duty for Aberdeen ! Our hardest of those matches was always that against Edinburgh, but our happiest outing was to St Andrews. There the evening sing-song was an event in itself. The St Andrews men were rich in tradition as in musical talent, and Anderson's recital of " Andrew Machrie " was one of the highlights. But we, too, made our humble contribution to the programme. Frankie would entertain with his " Ada Serenade "; Bruce would give " The lum hat wantin' a croon "; the outside-right was certain to provide some original item; and the student choruses were certain to be supplemented by " I wouldn't leave my little wooden hut for you-oo-oo " and " When we are married we'll have sausages for tea." On the homeward journey the match was thoroughly reviewed and the late train brought us once again into the Granite City. Another inter-varsity match was chalked up, to be remembered down the years.

Although I retained my status as amateur throughout my playing days, I had the privilege and pleasure during 1908-10 of finding my place along with the professionals in the Aberdeen Football Team League eleven. The comradeship of the field was an important part of my liberal education. The warning of a fellow student that an amateur would not fit in with the professionals proved quite untrue, and my association with the clubmates on Pittodrie's classic ground has remained among my treasured memories. Who could have had a finer type of captain than we had in Donald Coleman? and who among players had a bigger heart and a more boyish and impish spirit than the incorrigible defender Jock Hume? The team of those days included the famous left wing partnership of Charlie O'Hagan and Willie Lennie, while in the half-back line we had the stalwarts " Bowfer " Low, Geordie Wilson and Jimmy McBoyle. Bobby Simpson, our strongest finisher, partnered me on the right wing, with Paddy Travers among other artistes in the forward line. The goalkeepers of my time were Rab MacFarlane, Sandy Mutch, Arthur King and George Anderson. The fiercest battle in my recollection was a League match at Dens Park, when O'Hagan and Lawson of Dundee had to retire to the pavilion for unallowable toughness which led to a month's suspension. Dundee had most of the game, but in the last minute I anticipated a perfect cross from Lennie and placed the ball in the back of the net to equalise the score and save a point. An Aberdeen fan, in wild enthusiasm, rushed on to the playing-field, and after embracing me tenderly, raised his hand in benediction over the head of the Divinity student and said, " God bless you, MacEchern, more and more for ever and ever, Amen." Never before or since has a more sincere blessing been pronounced upon me. In April 1910 I was invited from Inverness to meet the Directors of the Club in the Pittodrie old pavilion, where they presented me with a handsome gold watch. In 1954 the watch is still ticking, a continuing souvenir of those days of happy comradeship.

Although my recollection of the classes and of the work in the University classroom is not quite so fresh, I suppose that I ought to make some reference to this department of University life. After all, the professors had some part in our making! The scholarship of Sir William Ramsay commanded our respect even if he did fail to appreciate the class presentation of an enormous turkey on the last day of the term before Christmas. We meant well; and we felt at the time that the professor might have been a little more generous in his acceptance of it. Johnnie Harrower, who occupied the Chair of Greek, did so with dignity and appeared as one who had stepped immediately from the Acropolis. To the honours students his lectures were a delight, and even to the humbler majority who aimed only at an ordinary degree his introduction to the works of Phidias and other Greek sculptors was a real fascination. It was difficult to adjudge his sense of humour when, without a smile, he made this announcement: "This, of course, is only a test examination. You have still three weeks before the Degree examination; and some of you who have made NO marks in the test may make TWICE as many in the Degree!" Nevertheless it is to the Greek classroom that I trace my still unfulfilled desire to visit the Islands and look upon the ruins of the glory that was Greece.

In the class of Moral Philosophy I aspired to a prize for an essay on "The Moral Judgement." Before handing it in to the professor I was informed by a classmate that I had spelt the title incorrectly. In self-defence I hastily wrote at the foot of the cover page: "Please note that I have spelt judgement throughout according to Shakespeare." On the return of the essay, which did not attain to the figure of the prize-winner, the professor had scribbled: "And quite right, too!" No wonder he became later the Chancellor of an English University!

Professor Niven of the class of Natural Philosophy was recognised as one of the great experimenters and teachers of our day. He was severe but very just. One of his class, absent on many occasions through illness but always miraculously restored to fitness by Saturday, failed to satisfy the professor that he had either attended with regularity or performed the work of the class. He was accordingly refused a "Sign-up," which meant a further session in the class; so, accompanied by a comrade to give him moral support, the hopeful High-lander called upon Mr Niven, who listened to his tale of woe and then said: "You cannot expect me to furnish you with a certificate if you have neither attended the class nor performed the work satisfactorily. You cannot expect me to give you a parchment to the effect that you have completed a course of study in this subject and then allow you to go out into the world and teach others." "But," interposed the intrepid opportunist, "it is not my intention to be a teacher." "And, pray, what is your intention ?" "I'm going to be a minister, sir." The professor, fixing on his eyeglass, dipped his pen in the ink and wrote out a certificate. Folding it up very carefully and handing it to the delighted student he said, with a characteristic twinkle in his eyes, "You know quite enough Natural Philosophy to preach the Gospel !" The student is to-day one of the most successful ministers in the Church of Scotland. Many years later, when I had the pleasure of meeting the professor's widow in Braemar, I related this incident and she agreed that it was quite typical of her beloved. From the distance we salute our old professors and we appreciate, more than at the time of our studies, all that we owe to them. And when, in course of time, further academic honours were laid upon them, none rejoiced with a greater joy than those who once had sat under them in the classrooms of instruction.

I hope that I shall not be charged with a sense of irreverence when I relate the following incident. It was on the occasion of the late Sir George Adam Smith's first sermon in the College Chapel as Principal-elect. On the previous day I had distinguished myself in a small way in an inter-varsity football match and on the Sunday I happened to be the student reader at the service. Among the congregation were several of the football team, and whether this fact was uppermost in my subconscious mind I know not; but what followed is true. In the New Testament lesson I had to read "And the Holy Ghost came down upon them." Imagine my horror when I heard the words come from my own lips: "And the Goaly Post came down upon them." The Principal, Sir George Adam Smith, recorded this in his own diary, and twenty years later, when I came as minister to Aberdeen, he mentioned it to me as a fine specimen of spoonerism.

There was only one other occasion, as far as I know, when I found myself tongue-tied in quoting Scripture. What I had intended saying was: "The people were too busy measuring

Jerusalem." But my threefold effort was something like this :
" The people were too mizzy . . ." " The people were too
juicy . . ." " The people were too boozy jessering Meru-
salem ! " When all my sermons were forgotten, my
congregation in Colombo remembered that one sentence.
The former of those incidents came back to my memory
when I preached a year or two ago in the Old Chapel under
the hoary crown of King's.

STUDENT DIGGINGS

Last autumn, when in Aberdeen, I made my way to number
33 Holburn Road to call upon an old lady in order that I
might give her my belated but appreciative greetings. Mrs
Mozley had been my landlady during three of my happiest
college years. Before going to 24 Albyn Grove—the corner
house with the veteran aspidistra in the window—I had spent
one winter session in the Divinity Residence in the Spital.
Such a hall had many advantages : it was no more than three
minutes' walk from the University Athletic Grounds, and we
were well catered for at the modest figure of fourteen shillings
per week. The Residence was one of Professor Cowan's pet
schemes and great was his disappointment when W. D. Fyfe
and I announced our intention of going into lodgings when
the new session commenced. But we both felt that there
were certain disadvantages in that cloistered life : chiefly we
experienced a certain cramping tendency in the continuous
contact with our fellow divines and the unfailing topic of
Church of Scotland. We wanted to breath more deeply and
to broaden our outlook on life and things in general. Thus
it was that in 1908 we found ourselves at No. 27, in close
proximity to Mr Cowell's shop, where we bought our evening
paper and the weekly *Gem*, and on high occasions supplemented
our table with a large bottle of Hay's No. 1 lemonade at one
penny. Our sitting-room was comfortably furnished even to
the extent of a rocking chair, and we were more fortunate
than many of our fellow students in that we had an excellent

[*Photo by John Stewart, Inchmahoe.*

STORMY SEAS OFF CLABBACH BAY, ISLAND OF COLL

[Photo by C. V. A. MacEchern.

KIRKMABRECK PARISH CHURCH

[To face page 25.

piano, of which we made full use. If I was the pianist, W. D. was the soloist; and if in his quiet moods he selected " Drink to me only " or Stevenson's " Requiem," he invariably worked up to a more boisterous pitch, producing from his repertoire " The Galloping Major," " Come, my lad, and be a Soldier " and " Yipiaddy." But " The Twin Duet " was our party piece when we were invited to an evening with friends. The landlady was indulgent and sympathetic with us in our musical revels, for her own son Charlie had now left school and was apprenticed to the leading music firm in Union Street. Some years later he went to South Africa in the same profession, and in the First World War he joined up and made the supreme sacrifice in France. Charlie's little sister Lena was still at school and at the stage when we could pull her hair and gladden her heart with a pennyworth of coconut chunks from across the road; but already she was a capable help in her home, and she continues a dutiful daughter to her mother, whose advanced years are cheered and made pleasant by her loving care.

It has often puzzled me how we students were housed and fed so comfortably at the unbelievable weekly cost of eleven shillings each. Mrs Mozley took a real motherly interest in her two students, and she rose to the occasion when we introduced quite an innovation in the nature of a little party for some of our wee friends in the neighbourhood. Very thoughtfully she supplemented the extra cakes and pastries we had provided with some original dainties which added to the attractiveness of our humble supper table. The party was at five o'clock, and fond mamas made their appearance about seven to escort the young guests home. The idea of the juvenile party was W. D.'s; he was rich in novelties, of which this was but one. Another original idea of his was the presentation of a dozen tickets to a young ladies' school on the occasion of the Students' Concert in the Music Hall. The school was reputed to be very correct and its discipline exemplary, and we thought that this concert by the University students would be a healthy diversion for the young ladies. In due course we both presented ourselves before the Principal of the school with the tickets. At first she appeared to be horrified at our proposal and looked down her nose at us with serious suspicion. Fyfe, however—always irresistible—was equal to the occasion, and proudly he laid his trump card, just when I was certain that our mission was proving a fiasco. " But, of course," he assured the Principal, " we are *Divinity* students." But the look in her eyes seemed to ask, " And does that make it any better—or worse ? " On the evening of the concert the twelve young ladies were seated along with one of the mistresses in the second row of the back gallery. Recently in the extreme south-west of Scotland I met a lady who introduced herself to me as one of the twelve flappers who attended and enjoyed the recital.

A UNIVERSITY TORCHLIGHT

IN my own days at the University the Gala Day for the Hospitals had not yet been conceived, but we had our own great days. Perhaps the most outstanding was the triennial Rectorial Election with its accompanying Torchlight. Older brothers had often told me of those high occasions at Edinburgh, most famous of all being the Lord Goschen Rectorial; so when my turn came to participate in such a function at Aberdeen I was all prepared for it. Sir Frederick Treves was the chosen one, and on the occasion of his first visit as Lord Rector—an office which Sir John Orr said recently was the highest honour to which a Scotsman could aspire—he was given a right hearty welcome from an enthusiastic studentdom. Are there any of the old Ritchieites who still remember their Battle Song as they marched in irregular column to the Peasemeal Fight ? It was sung to the tune of " My Bonnie."

" Treves has been over the ocean,
    Treves has been over the sea ;
  He's now got a queer sort of notion
    Lord Rector he's going to be.

Treves 'll go back o'er the ocean,
  Or drown himself far out at sea ;
For each one has now got the notion
  That Ritchie's the man for me."

Nevertheless Treves, whom his opponents described in one of their posters as " the stop-gap of a conglomeration of irresponsible nonentities," was eventually returned at the top of the poll. I like to recall his pleasant anecdote told by him at a students' symposium on the occasion of our Quater-centenary Celebration. He related how on an earlier occasion he had been appointed as one of the co-examiners for the Medical Finals. Electing to come from London by steamer, he fell in with a student of the bright irresponsible type. This student wore a college " Blue " and a straw-basher of that period. In course of conversation he told Sir Frederick that he was bound for Aberdeen to sit his Final. He also volunteered the information that along with the professor there was a fellow who was called a co-examiner. Of course that didn't trouble this student. The " Co," as he familiarly called him, knew less about the subject than did the examinee. The latter was fresh off the rails, while the co-examiner was some old josser who had long ago forgotten all that he might ever have known of the subject. Treves, on hearing all this, resolved to leave the fellow in ignorance as to his identity ; but next forenoon in the examination hall the full " Blue " in his turn presented himself, to find to his utter confusion that his voyaging companion of the previous day was no other than the co-examiner ! Without pretending to recognise the youth Sir Frederick commenced : " Good morning, Mr ——, I am the co-examiner. Of course there is not much point in me putting any questions to you. I am but an old josser and you are fresh off the rails. You know far more about the subject than I do." The student felt himself growing smaller and smaller. Failure stared him in the face and he had but one wish—that the floor might open up and swallow him. But the eminent doctor put him out of further pain, as only a doctor could do, by adding in conclusion : " So I shall ask no questions. You have passed the examination !" The story, doubtless a figment of his imagination, was received with hilarious applause from the student audience whom Sir Frederick was addressing, and later in the evening we joined in singing " For he's a jolly good fellow."

Another speech-making incident comes to mind—the speech made by Sir Andrew Carnegie at the same celebrations. It was towards the conclusion of the famous Strathcona Banquet, at which we had listened to numerous orations occasioned by an imposing toast list. Carnegie had to propose the " City of Aberdeen "; but at that late stage of the long proceedings we were in no mood for any further speeches, and the steel magnate was wise enough to know this. He stepped forward to the megaphone, holding in his hand a sheaf of typed foolscap manuscript. The students, seeing it, groaned ; but Sir Andrew, holding the manuscript aloft and waving it high above his head (which was not very high), exclaimed : " My lords, ladies and gentlemen, I rise to propose the toast of the City of Aberdeen. Here it is. You will read it all in to-morrow morning's paper . . . ' The City of Aberdeen ' ! " And no speech that evening was received with greater heartiness.

There was an unwritten law at Lodge Walk—the head-quarters of the City Police—that on the occasion of a Torchlight Procession the students were given the freedom of the city, and the members of the force were given strict in-junction to hide themselves until the frolics of the masqueraders were past and over. All along the route of procession the street lights one by one went out. This added to the effect of the long line of blazing torches held aloft as we proceeded, to the delight of the spectators, along Union Street, up Albyn Place, down Rosemount and back to the quadrangle at Marischal. There the torches were flung into the common heap to form a wondrous bonfire round which, in our fantastic garbs of every nationality and period, we danced and sang. At a late hour the last embers flickered ; in twos and threes we betook ourselves to our several lodgings ; another Rectorial was ended, to be rehearsed in after years, when two or three of the old students forgathered in distant parts of the far-flung empire or in the cold grey city by the sea. As we look back, let R. F. Murray, the student poet of St Andrews, express our sentiment:

> " Now we are old and sensible men
> And wrinkles our brows embellish;
> And I fear we never shall relish again
> The things that we used to relish;
> And I fear we never again shall go
> The wind and the weather scorning,
> For a twelve-mile walk in the frozen snow
> At one o'clock in the morning.
> Out by Cameron, in by the Grange,
> And to bed as the moon descended;
> To you and to me there has come a change,
> The days of our youth are ended."

> " Life has not since been wholly vain,
> And now I bear
> Of wisdom plucked from joy and pain
> Some slender share.
> But howsoever rich the gain,
> I'd lay it down,
> To feel upon my back once more
> The old Red Gown."

A THEATRE TRAGEDY RECALLED

THE present generation is too young to have known the Great Lafayette, one of the supreme artistes among the world's illusionists. I myself witnessed his fascinating performance once only—and it was his last; for one of the saddest of all music-hall tragedies rang down the curtain upon his illustrious career.

It was at the second house on the concluding evening of his show in the Edinburgh Empire; the great theatre was crowded and we had come to the close of his dramatic act,

" The Lion's Bride." The scene was an eastern harem and the young heroine had been flung into the cage occupied by the African lion. As the fierce monster sprang upon her, her lover, Lafayette himself, dashed on to the stage upon his beautiful black charger and fired a shot at the attacking animal. At the firing of that shot something like a paper serviette came floating down upon the stage alight and in a moment the flimsy curtains and cushions in the harem became ablaze. Next moment the safety curtain came slowly down, but so many spectacular thrills had preceded this last act that the members of the audience were under the impression that the firing of the harem was the dramatic conclusion of the act. Some of them had already risen and were leaving the theatre before the horror dawned upon us that the stage was actually on fire.

By some unfortunate hitch in the mechanism the safety curtain stuck about four feet from the stage floor, and through the open space we could see figures on the stage dashing about excitedly amidst what was already a raging inferno. I remember a tall negro stooping beneath the curtain and signalling to the orchestra, who immediately commenced to play, in order, I suppose, to calm the audience ; but the flames were already sweeping from the stage over the heads of the players into the auditorium.

There was no panic, and the audience, numbering close upon two thousand, were pressing their way through various exits, I myself among them, minus my coat and hat. Outside the rain was falling and the street was thronged with spectators as the fire raged. Rumours were rife and these were not exaggerated, for in the earliest hours of the morning when the fire brigade had controlled the blaze it was discovered that eleven of the cast, all trapped behind the scenes, had perished, among them the Great Lafayette himself. He had dashed back to the stage to rescue his beautiful pony, and with him died also the pony and the lion. The last act of this man of mystery was the most mysterious of all, for the cause of the conflagration was never determined.

Some years later, in a theatre in Colombo, Ceylon, I met

another illusionist of fame—Carter the Great, an intimate friend of Houdini. At the time of the Edinburgh Empire fire he was appearing in his own show somewhere in England and he immediately telegraphed his profound sympathy with the surviving members of the Lafayette troupe. He also offered to stand in with what help he could, and later took over " The Lion's Bride " as his own. The lion for his act, he told me, he bought from the King of Italy. It was a beautiful specimen of fifteen years and was as tame as a pussy cat. Indeed, one afternoon he invited my wife to enter the cage and the animal purred pleasantly as she stroked his chin.

Lafayette was buried in the Scottish capital three days after the tragedy. The streets were lined as Edinburgh had never seen them before or since when that prince of his profession was laid to rest.

A HEBRIDEAN SUMMER VACATION

HAVING cleared the last hurdle for my M.A. degree, I set forth for the Island of Coll to enjoy a real and, as I imagined, a deserved holiday. The only drawback to the full happiness of that summer for myself was the fact that, before returning to the University to commence my divinity studies, I had to sit my Presbyterial examination. As the retention of my Fraser Bursary depended on my passing that examination, I spent many hours in preparation for that ordeal; for the Presbytery was known to include in its numbers not a few scholarly ministers, some of whom would be my examiners. I renewed my acquaintance with the Shorter Catechism, brushed up my Greek and covered a good part of the third Gospel. The weeks passed all too quickly and on the appointed day I sailed for Tobermory. Stormy weather brought the S.S. " Fingal " into the sheltered bay three hours late, and accordingly the meeting of the Fathers and Brethren commenced at 2 P.M. instead of at 11 A.M. The ordinary business being concluded, my hour arrived. " Bring in the student,"

I heard the Moderator command, and I came forth as a lamb to the slaughter. " Mr Smith will test your theological attainments, Mr Macpherson will examine you in Greek and Mr Macgregor in Bible knowledge." All three were held in the highest respect for their scholarship. Mr Smith then coughed in a professional manner before commencing his questions ; but ere he had time to utter a word the door was flung open and the beadle announced in a stentorian voice, " Gentlemen, the boat is round the Point ! " This intimation was as though the end of the world had come. Confusion reigned supreme. " We must catch the boat ; we must not lose our boat. . . . But what about the student ? " " Ask him a question," instructed the Moderator ; but the minister of Ardnamurchan could not for the life of him think of a question. Then suddenly he blurted out, " What is man's chief end ? " This was too easy, and proudly I recited the answer in the Catechism. " Very good, very good ; that will do. Moderator, I beg to move that his Trials be sustained." And sustained they were ; a certificate to that effect was placed in my hand and the Benediction was pronounced. Then followed a hurried rush down to the pier, where the S.S. " Hebrides " was lowering the gangway, and soon we were once again making our way to the Islands. Mr Smith was the first of the Presbyters to address me on board. " I am thinking we had better give you a few more questions, young man." " I think, sir," I answered respectfully but firmly, " it will be unnecessary. I have in my pocket a certificate to the effect that my Trials have been duly sustained." Ever since I have had a soft side for the Presbytery of Mull !

I think it was in that same summer that some excitement prevailed in the Island over the publication of the banns of marriage of a certain popular Islander. It looked as if there was going to be a double wedding in the family, until the minister discovered that the banns handed in indicated that both brothers were proposing to marry the same sweet maid ! To proclaim both sets of banns, however, struck the minister as being somewhat Gilbertian ; and although it was but ten minutes until the hour of the service, his University athletics were of a sufficiently recent date to permit him dash up the hillside to the croft and return in time. The parishioners were already assembling around the church and there was some speculation as to the meaning of the unusual sight of the minister covering the ground in true cross-country style. But well he could do it; had he not distinguished himself at college in such events !

The interview with the lady was of short duration. She could not decide which of the brothers it was to be; each had his distinctive merit and attraction, and eventually she agreed to allow the minister to make the fatal choice on her behalf. Like a Solomon he spoke: " For two years you have been courting Alistair ? " " True." " And everybody is expecting you to marry Alistair ? " " True." " And Alistair is expecting you to marry him ? " " True." " Then Alistair let it be." And so it came about that, when the minister entered the pulpit fifteen minutes later, the banns were proclaimed. And the following Wednesday the " also-ran " appeared, without the suggestion of a grudge, in the role of best man at the wedding of the season.

These are but recollections; for now, when the wedding bells ring forth their joyous note, the bride and bridegroom are the children of a new generation. But with Martial we say :—

> " Hoc est
> Vivere bis, vita posse priore frui."

MY DAY OF ORDINATION

> " *All are now in country manses,*
>   *Hebrew vexes them no more ;*
> *But the fattest living never*
>   *Can bring back those days of yore.*"
>
> —Student Song.

LOOKING back over my successive ministries in five parishes— four in Scotland and one overseas in Colombo, Ceylon, the diary which covers my first year as an ordained minister is of particular interest and instructiveness. After a strenuous assistantship in the parish of St Cuthbert's, Edinburgh, under the wise and kindly guidance of Dr G. D. S. Duncan, I was elected minister of that lovely parish in the heart of the Kyles of Bute—Tighnabruaich. I had survived the ordeal of preaching on a short leet of no fewer than SIX; and in that connection I had written to my brother John, who was already happily settled in a parish, suggesting that he might be in a position to offer me some useful advice as to how best to comport myself as a candidate. He sent me back by reply a briefly worded postcard: "Preach the Gospel and shake hands with the Beadle." And did I? On the Sunday I preached three Gospel sermons, and on Monday morning, before departing on the "Texa," I made a point of calling on the beadle and heartily shook hands with him. "I liked that candidate," he said afterwards; "he gie's ye a graun' haunshake!" When the voting came on, by a narrow majority I was elected. The handshake had done it, and my diary contains this simple entry: "Festus dies."

On the morning of the induction I stepped off the "Columba" down the gangway at Auchenlochan feeling very pleased with myself and with all the world. I immediately noticed a stalwart figure whom I recognised as one of the worshippers when I preached as a candidate. He came forward to the foot of the gangway and extended his open hand. I laid down my suit case and grasped the proffered fist warmly. "Thank you for your kind welcome. You are the first to shake hands with me on my arrival." I then proceeded ashore and, ere the setting of the sun, word had gone round the parish from Ardlamont to Glen Caladh that the new minister was a "smairt yin." For the piermaster had merely extended his hand for the tuppence as pier dues, and the new incumbent in response had given him a handshake and passed on! "Aye," remarked the blacksmith when told of it, "but ye maun mind that he's had seven years in Aberdeen!"

The Presbytery of Bute inducted and ordained me with

impressive dignity; was not Dr King Hewison the Moderator, supported by stalwarts of the kirk such as John M. Dickie of New Rothesay, who was to prove such a counsellor and friend in coming days, and Saunders of Kingarth as clerk and the veteran MacPhee of Kilfinan? In the evening the customary social welcome was held in the hall attached to the Royal Hotel, whose proprietor was my much respected elder Mr Robert Duncan. It was he who on one occasion clean bowled a London visitor who had said to him, "Mr Duncan, yours must be a very quiet life down here. Do you never come up to London to see the sights there?" "Oh, no," replied the much-travelled veteran, "the sights of London come up here and we see them fine!" The induction programme included some fourteen speeches and I resolved that, in order to get home within elders' hours, four minutes must be the maximum for each of the orations. In order to support and emphasise my authority as chairman I borrowed a table bell from the hotel, and as each speaker's time-limit elapsed I pressed the knob of the bell, which sounded loud and imperative. Every time I did so there were loud guffaws and applause from the back-seaters, and it was only on the following day that I discovered the secret of their mirth: the bell was one which did duty ordinarily in the bar of the hotel, and as one facetious farmer said to me afterwards, "Man, minister, you rang that bell as if to the manner born!"

I shall not record any of the speeches made at that induction social, for the addresses made on such occasions are all very much alike. It is the one occasion when a liar's licence is granted to the ministerial speakers, and for the most part they take full advantage of it. The young minister feels himself rising on wings and is conscious of a golden halo about his head. It is his one crowded hour of glory; for the halo swiftly passes and the welcome superlatives fade into the light of common day. I have often wished since that I had been married at the time so that my wife might have heard the flatteries paid me!

I was particularly happy that day in the friends who came from afar to see me "placed" and whose presence and counsel helped to give me courage and confidence. Among them were my own parents, proud in seeing the third of their sons to be ordained and inducted; my brother John, my sister, my very great friend the minister of St Cuthbert's; Miss Stewart, the deaconess in Edinburgh; my former colleagues Douglas Bruce, now of Buenos Aires, Robert Sneddon, who became minister of St James's, Portobello, and W. D. Fyfe of beloved memory, with whom, while we were students, I had shared the happiest of lodgings in Aberdeen. Ordination comes only once—it is a day to be remembered. A few months later I made this entry in my diary: " Received to-day my first stipend as minister. There will not be much of it left when I have paid all the bills outstanding ! " Nor was there—nor has there been ever since.

It is always a real pleasure for me to visit that parish in the Kyles. Have I forgotten the kindliness with which the congregation overlooked my early mistakes, and the indulgent encouragement which was given me by old and young alike ? The old church, picturesquely set on the hill, is no longer being used for worship; nor is my old manse now the minister's residence. But forty years have not allowed the happiness of those days to fade. Sometimes I hear the music of the burn which was a feature of the garden, and the merry voices of the children passing down the brae from school keep sounding in my dreams of long ago. Perhaps it is Tighnabruaich that has made C. F. Smith's verse one of my favourite quotations :—

> " ' Times . . . they pass,' said Murphy,
> ' The fair and the foul weather,
> The good times and the bad,
> They all pass together
> Like a steersman's trick that's ended
> Or a blown-out squall ;
> An' the times a man remembers . . .
> They're the best times of all.' "

MALTA IN THE FIRST GREAT WAR

War Hospitals in Malta, 1915-1917

THE hospital ship " Gloucester Castle " landed me among a draft of R.A.M.C. upon the Island of Malta, lying in the quiet blue waters of the tideless Mediterranean. Since then I have seen them in their angry fury—the Euroclydon blowing, which drove St Paul to his historic shipwreck upon that same island, then known as Melita. There, on the fringe of war, we were brought face to face with the price paid by the broken bodies and the wasted health of a great company who had gone forth in the pride of youth and in the strength of manhood. In the summer of 1916 our hospital accommodation reached the figure of 27,000 beds, and preparation was being made to increase this to 35,000. Serving first in the hospital of Floriana —in peace time an infantry barracks—I found myself happy in my comrades. While on duty little opportunity was afforded for argument ; but the fate of empires was settled in our own marquee in the evenings and after " lights out." Scott, as his name suggested, was strong in metaphysics, while Williams —" historian "—was still talking long after his tent-mates were asleep. Two years scattered our marquee over the island and farther afield ; but in 1917, at my wedding in the Scots kirk of Valletta, I had the honour of a guard from the old crowd, Private Smith, now sporting three stripes as sergeant-cook, in command, and Sykes smiling by his side. I wonder where Sykes is ? His bugling had few rivals, and his sounding of " Reveille " had a note of compulsion about it which required no supplementary " show-a-leg."

I suppose it is perfectly safe at this distant date to recall an incident and confess my breach of King's Regulations. On the occasion of my first visit to the Scots kirk I introduced myself to the preacher, Rev. Donald Campbell of Greenock, who insisted on my accompanying him to dinner at the Osborne Hotel. He had forgotten, however, that the stringency of military regulations refused to admit even a corporal to the same table with men of commissioned rank. But two Scotsmen are equal to any occasion, and divesting myself of my khaki uniform in the padre's bedroom, I speedily emerged wearing the discarded clericals of Mr Campbell and fraternising at the festal board with consuls, commanders and colonels, dignified but very human officers whose " brass hats " I had seen glitter in the outer hall. The dinner was excellent— the Maltese chefs are wonderful; and later in the evening, once again in the King's uniform, I returned to my tent in Floriana in time for " lights out." I related my dinner experience with every detail to envious and critical comrades; and as we turned over " to sleep, perchance to dream," the last word was spoken by a Paisley humorist chewing a raw onion —his nightly practice: " If any o' you boys is hungry, jist help yersels tae mair puddin' an' custaird ! "

Among many provisions for the entertainment of the wounded the Scottish church hall was thrown open as a tea-room and reading centre. For some time my fiancée was in charge there with a band of willing lady helpers. I recollect helping to arrange a Scottish picnic and asking a young trooper whether he thought he would manage to attend it. His reply was full of meaning: " Will A' no' ? A'm no' me if A'm no' there ! " I had the pleasure of delivering a number of lectures to the troops, chiefly on Scottish subjects. One was billed on the camp notice-board, " An Hour wi' the Jocks "; and when I took the platform, a voice from the very back of the great marquee greeted me with, " Come awa', Aiberdeen," as probably it had often shouted to me from the touchline at Pittodrie. At another lecture a picture was thrown upon the lantern screen, a photograph of Nazareth. " By Jove," said a smart London soldier, " ain't that just like the pictures of old London ? " An observant and argumentative Jock, pointing to a camel in the foreground of the picture, remarked, " Ha'e ye ever seen camels in London ? " Back came the answer, " No, but I've seen many a Scotsman with the 'ump."

It was the saddest of my duties as Chaplain that brought me each evening at the hour of sunset to the cemetery of Pieta —a beautiful resting-place for our dead heroes, with the willows hanging gracefully where the firing party stood. The muffled drums and the solemn music of the Dead March told you that the gun carriages were approaching. On each coffin there rested the khaki helmet of the sleeping warrior. A number of passers-by gathered; the children stopped their play and seemed to understand; the men uncovered as the procession passed up to the gates. After the short service three sharp volleys were fired and the " Last Post " was sounded. Then we turned away, not sorrowing as men without hope, but with a great pride in our hearts and leaving on each grave a wreath of flowers, " Malta's tribute to dead heroes—with deepest sympathy." And we thought of those far away who were waiting even yet in hope, those who would know before the setting of another sun that the crown of victory was won; and we prayed for them, as we stood at the open grave— prayed that God would strengthen their faith and give them courage in the time of their heart's breaking to look up to Him and that, realising the faith of Christ, they might possess the peace of Christ. As we came away from Pieta, the band now playing a jubilant song, the lines of Henry Warnoch came to me again :—

> " Life is not all.
> If life were all,
> Where were the recompense
> For all our tears ?
> If life were all,
> How might we bear
> Our poor heart's grief,
> Our partings frequent
> And our pleasures brief ?
> The cup pressed to the lips
> Then snatched away
> Were scarce worth looking on
> If life were all."

Surely, if anything might convince, it were the glorious offering unto death for a great cause by men on the very threshold of their manhood.

DEPARTURE FROM MALTA

Too soon our visit to this sacred Isle
Of light and old romance
Comes to a close;
Too soon the shadows of departing day
Enshroud its battlements
And daylight goes.
To-morrow's light will flood this landscape o'er,
But not for us the joy
Of recent days;
The moving ship will bear us far away
Where we shall miss the sun's refulgent rays;
And in the darkened night around the glow
Of cosy fire at home
We'll live again,
These pleasant days beside the sapphire sea
And sweet remembrances
That banished pain.
Too soon our visit to the sacred Isle
Of earliest hopes and dreams
Comes to an end;
But to the Future—whatsoe'er be lost—
Some things that cannot die,
That Past will lend.

IN THE ANCIENT KINGDOM OF KINTYRE

SHORT versus Long Ministries is a subject of recurring debate;
but after six years in my first parish, much though I loved it
and its kindly people, I felt that I was ready for pastures new.
I had not forgotten what a minister of wide experience once
said to me: "If you can make anything of a parish in six
years, you will be ready for a change; and if you cannot, the
parishioners will be ready for a change." So I came to

TIGHNABRUAICH PARISH CHURCH

[*To face page* 41.

Campbeltown. Here again my election was by a small majority. There is never any certainty as to how the voting in a church election will go; a triviality may be a deciding factor. Discussing the merits and demerits of the various candidates in my first election shortly afterwards, I ventured to ask a friend what it was in myself that had appealed to the congregation; but I was not quite prepared for his reply. "There was one thing that weighed in your favour: you were the only one among the candidates who, when preaching on the leet, prayed for the best man to be elected. And, of course, we knew fine whom you had in mind!" In the Campbeltown election one vote at least was recorded in my favour on quite erroneous grounds. When I left my hotel for the morning service the church bell commenced to ring. Thinking that it must be almost time for the service I accelerated my pace, and as I climbed the hill to the church I overtook several of the congregation and politely bowed as I shot past them. One good lady resolved there and then to give me her vote. "Any minister," she declared, "who goes to the church at that pace means business." In my candidature at Campbeltown I felt that I had a decided advantage over my fellow preachers—a running start, as I expressed it to myself; for on the Town Cross I read the names of two of my own clan.

Hec · est · crux ·
domini · Yvari · M · K · Eachyrna ·
quodam · rectoris · de · Kylregan ·
et · domini · Andree · nati · ajus ·
rectoris · de · Kilchoman · qui · hanc
crucem · fieri · faciebat ·

Translation of Inscription—

This is the cross of Master (or Reverend) Yvar Mac Eachern, once rector of Kilregan, and Master Andrew, his son, rector of Kilcoman, who erected this cross.

———

This cross was erected about A.D. 1500.

In my ministry in the Lowland charge I was happy in making many new friends and in being supported in my work by many zealous workers. Campbeltown at that time was a collegiate charge—never an ideal situation, as was experienced by one of my successors; and the General Assembly recently separated the two charges. I went there as assistant and successor to the Rev. Walter Strang, who had been minister of the charge for forty years; and he and Mrs Strang, along with three of their daughters, continued to reside within the burgh and proved of invaluable help to me in all my work. In a little book which I published while there—" The Book of Old Castlehill "—published by T. & A. Constable Ltd., I included a brief tribute to Mr Strang by the Very Rev. Canon John Macdonald of the Roman Catholic Church. Concerning my predecessor Canon Macdonald wrote: " His magnificent manliness, his courage and his sympathy, left no room for prejudice. I rejoiced in his friendship. An hour with him was better than the best tonic. His outlook was wide as the heavens, and in his world there was room for everyone. He was consistently cheery, and his radiant mirth infected those with whom he came in contact. His was a personality in the district. We miss him sorely, but his influence and his message remain."

My ministerial colleagues in the other churches in Campbeltown were the Rev. Mr Brown of the Longrow, retiring and studious; the Rev. B. B. Blackwood, along with whom I was to play in the Academicals football club; the Rev. Charles Maclean of Lorne Street, with whom I exchanged pulpits many times in the year; the Rev. Norman Mackenzie of the Highland parish, and the Rev. P. W. Miller of the Free Church. If, on entering my second parish, I felt confident in the task facing me, I was shaken in that confidence when on an early Saturday forenoon I dismounted from my bicycle to speak to a stone-breaker by the roadside. " You'll be the new minister of the Lowland Church ? " he surmised. I acknowledged that I was; and then, leaning on his stone hammer, he said rather disparagingly, " Well, let me tell you that the new ministers are not like the old ones. Man, we had

Dr Russell and Hector Mackinnon. Can you find a minister like Hector nowadays ? Man, I tell you I've seen Hector sweetin' in the pulpit ! " Years later, when in the pulpit of the Scots Kirk in Colombo in a temperature of 95 degrees in the shade, I recalled that speech and felt that at last I was a great preacher !

My happiest recollection of Campbeltown days is the great bazaar which we held on the first two days of the year 1921. It was a season of unemployment and depression. But as the day approached the enthusiasm rose, and at the conclusion of the bazaar I had the happiness of announcing that the drawings had amounted to the handsome sum of £1,197. The bazaar was declared open by Her Grace the Dowager Duchess of Argyll, whose residence was at Macharioch, Southend. I was much encouraged in my ministry in Campbeltown by her interest and help. She was enthusiastic in connection with the Girl Guide movement, and before leaving I had the pleasure of receiving from her hands the silver Thanks Badge of the Guides for services rendered. One of the last letters she wrote was to myself after I had been a couple of years in Ceylon, and it is typical of her warm interest in the work of the Church :—

MACHARIOCH, CAMPBELTOWN,
Jan. 8, 1924.

DEAR MR MACECHERN,

Before the year is any older I must write a line to wish you all happiness and blessing in 1924. I feel sure you are prospering in your new sphere of work, knowing the power and energy you bring into all you do ; and by this time I am sure you have made many friends in Ceylon. I miss much all your kind and able help in my undertakings, and when I had my school children's entertainment last week I remembered your delightful Punch and Judy Show and how much the little people enjoyed it. We are to have the Parade Service of the Guides next Sunday in the Lochend Church,

as all the churches must have their turn. Then later I am
going to present the Shield to the Campbeltown Girl Guides
which the different companies will compete for in the future,
but which will belong to Campbeltown only. With New
Year Greetings and kind regards to Mrs MacEchern.

Believe me,

Yours sincerely,

I. ARGYLL.

Cuthbert Bede in his book of legendary stories of the
West includes the following concerning one of my predecessors.
Before coming as minister to the Lowland parish, the Rev.
Daniel Kelly was for seventeen years in charge of the parish
of Southend. On one occasion Kelly went from Southend to
assist Dr MacNaughton at the sacramental services in
Campbeltown. It was arranged that Kelly should preach on
the Saturday and Dr MacNaughton on the Sunday. With
that in view, the former arrived at the Lowland manse on the
Friday, and in the evening, during the absence of the minister,
Kelly's eyes lighted upon a manuscript sermon on the study
table. It proved to be a most excellent sermon prepared by
the doctor with much care and study and intended for delivery
on the following Sunday. Kelly was a man of such prodigious
memory that a single reading of a sermon sufficed for its
committal to memory; as a result, on the following morning,
when Kelly had to preach, the intense surprise and chagrin
of the Doctor may be imagined when he heard his
friend delivering his own sermon, word for word, from the
beginning to the very end. Bede relates this under the plain
but honest headline: " How the Rev. Daniel Kelly stole a
sermon."

Among contributions for my Bazaar Book, to which I have
made reference, was an original unpublished poem by Neil
Munro.

MOTHER

YE were aye a rowdie laddie, Jock,
Since ever ye cam' hame,
Unco ill to bed at night,
And dour to wash and kaim.
It gave me many a he'rtbreak
To keep ye cosh and clean.
Now I'm he'rt-hale and sorry for't—
    Ye ken what I mean !

Your brither's deid in New Chapelle,
Your faither's in Kirkbride,
Ye're a' that's left that made for me
The joy o' Wanlochside.
I winna hae ye craven, mind,
Nor yet ower foolish keen ;
Let caution gang wi' courage, lad—
    Ye ken what I mean !

If ever ye come on a German chiel
That looks o' landward breed,
Some harum-scarum ne'er-dae-weel,
Blae een and lint-white heid,
That maybe played on the hairst-field
Like you when he was a wean ;
Let that yin by for his mither's sake—
    Ye ken what I mean !

Nane yet got me repinin',
Nor bendin' to my load ;
High heid in the market-toun,
Licht foot on the road !
There's nane to see Jean Cameron boo
But by her bed at e'en,
And I trust you're no' forgettin'—
    Ye ken what I mean !

I'm vexed noo when I think of it,
The way I let ye gang—
Just the wee clap on the shouther,
And nae fareweel harangue;
I couldna look ye in the face,
For the sun was in my een,
I'm a stupid auld Scots body—
　　Ye ken what I mean !

If Death were but a merchant-man
To strike a bargain wi',
The first at his booth in the Candleriggs
In the morn's morn would be me,
To swap him a fine auld withered brench
For a stubborn twig o' green—
But there !　I'm only haiverin'—
　　Ye ken what I mean !

THE PEARL OF THE ORIENT

". . . the real Ceylon, full of wild beauty, history and romance."—CLAIR RETTIE.

IN my book " Spicy Breezes from Sunny Ceylon," published in 1929, I recorded some happy impressions of the seven years of my sojourn there as minister of the Scots Kirk in Colombo; but the memories, which were fresh when I wrote, have not yet faded.　The Church of Scotland in the capital was an architectural gem, and the manse close beside it was a delightful residence, with its three acres of coconuts and plantains and a rich profusion of oriental shrubs.　Both church and manse had been built under the ministry of the Rev. Mr Dunn at a time when money among the Scots in the colony was plentiful. Mr Dainty, although not a Scot, presided over a choir, which we claimed to be the finest in the Orient.　Throughout the last two years of my ministry we broadcast a service once every month, and many letters of appreciation came to me and to the organist from planters in far out-stations. Among our soloists were Mr John Young, Mr John Murray, Mr Norrie, Mr Munro and Mr Robert Guthrie; and outstanding among the ladies were the Misses de Silva, Miss Gracie Keyt and Mrs Norrie. For a year and a half I conducted a monthly service at Kandy—surely the most picturesque town in Ceylon. It is situated some fifteen hundred feet above sea level and is distant from Colombo about seventy-five miles. I recall setting out on my first visit and hearing Mrs Southorn (Bella Sydney Wolff) saying, " I envy any one their first trip to Kandy." My wife and I were the guests of Mr and Mrs E. W. Keith on Kondesalle Estate, with whom also we made many a pleasant and exciting tour through the jungle to see leopards, elephants, little brown bears and the delicate-footed deer in their native haunts. On one trip a baby leopard, no bigger than a large cat, met us on the road and held up our car as it gazed in its bewilderment under the fierce glare of our head-lights. My wife would quickly have got out of the car and petted the creature, but the wiser counsel of our host prevailed, for the mother could not have been far distant.

The Scots padre was responsible also for services from time to time in the outlying parts of the plantations, and these were always a delight to look forward to. I specially recall my first visit to an up-country tea estate where we were the guests of Mr and Mrs Fred Stewart. Shortly before that I had officiated at their wedding in Colombo. The bride, who was well known in golfing circles in Scotland as Miss Lena Scroggie, was one up on me at the reception in the Galle Face Hotel. Before proposing the toast of Mr and Mrs Stewart I turned to the bride and asked, " Do you pronounce your name Scroggie or Scrogie ? " Promptly she replied, " I pronounce my name Stewart ! " That reception was attended by the Scottish planters from far and wide; and as the honey-mooners drove off in a shining Rolls-Royce we read on a placard hung from the back of the car one single word—BUNKERED ! That was but one of many enjoyable wedding occasions, for St Andrews was known as " The Wedding Kirk." There was another day when a Bibby liner, the

"Shropshire," brought to the East no fewer than fifteen blushing brides. At the luncheon after one of these marriages I made the suggestion that we should drink the health of the Captain of the ship. He was a cheery Irishman and his reply was to this effect: "Ladies and gentlemen, I have brought many a bride to these Eastern parts. On the present trip I have brought fifteen. But I will say this: that never before have I had the pleasure of bringing to Ceylon a more attractive, a more dazzling, a more charming young lady than the bride of the present occasion." When the loud and prolonged applause which greeted this generous sentiment had subsided, the Captain went on to add: "And I may say that for the past twelve years I have been making this identical speech at similar functions."

Not one hundred yards from the Scots Kirk manse was the residence of the Anglican Bishop of Colombo. That office was held by Bishop Copplestone, a brother of the Metropolitan of India. He was broad enough and kind enough to make the long journey to Kandy in order to come upon the platform at the diamond jubilee of the Presbytery of Ceylon and give us his episcopal greetings and blessing. Among the hobbies of his successor, Bishop Carpentier-Garnier, was whistling, at which he was a perfect artist. I believe that he had a genius also for Limerick verses. I myself indulged in that form of writing, and two of my efforts come to mind which I shall give here :—

> A woman whose voice was chromatic,
> Had a tongue that was quite acrobatic.
>   When it caught in the mangle,
>   She ceased from her jangle ;
> The silence was super-dramatic !

> Colombo's now crowded with buses,
> And every pedestrian cusses.
>   The drivers are brutal,
>   They never will tootle ;
> They kill you ; then ask what the fuss is !

THE LAND O' CAKES

AMONG memories which stand out relating to my period in Ceylon is the annual Caledonian Dinner, an outstanding function, at which His Excellency the Governor was invariably the guest of the evening. In 1925 the new Governor, Sir Hugh Clifford, set foot in the Island on the very day of the Scottish celebration and was given a rousing reception from the assembled members and guests. Two years earlier I had the honour of proposing " The Land o' Cakes," and here are the sentiments to which I gave expression :—

To-night from this evergreen land of coconuts and copra we salute the sterner glories of the " Land o' Cakes." It is a fitting toast, for the historian has told us that next to the love of God and his parents, it is the chief delight of Scotsmen that they love their country and their fellow-countrymen. The other day in the G.P.O. in Colombo, while waiting for a stamp, a youthful emigrant looked up and said, " Could you please tell me hoo mony stamps a'll hae to pit on a postcaird to Glesca ? " I asked him, " Are you a Scotsman ? " and with the greatest delight he replied, " Aye, a'm frae Glesca ; a wis born there a' ma days." To-night we are like the emigrant from Paisley, far from home. Unlike ourselves in these days of increasing dividends, he was down on his luck. But a travelling show invited him to take the place of the performing bear which had died. There being good pay attached to the job, Jock jumped at it. He learned his part, got inside the bear's skin and later in the day delighted the spectators. The showman then announced that the polar bear would now enter the cage of the fierce African lion. " Nae fears," whispered Jock in protest, " A'm awa' back to Paisley." But the showman insisted and, while the crowd sat breathless, they brought in the " bear," opened the gate of the cage and flung Jock inside. The lion roared savagely, sprang at the bear and opening its fierce jaws over Jock's head whispered, " Dinna be feared, Jock, A'm a Paisley man masel'."

To-night we are all Paisley buddies, or wee Aiberdonians, Highlanders from the North, or braw lads from the land of

Burns; and any who are not such are prepared to adopt Scottish nationality for the time being. We hail Caledonia, land of our sires, land of our youth, land of tender memories. Some here can turn to the next and say:

> We twa hae run aboot the braes
>   And pu'd the gowans fine,
> But we've wandered mony a weary foot
>   Sin' auld lang syne."

We take our sprig of heather, grown on some Highland hill, and use it to-night as a charm to induce the spell of the Land o' Cakes. Some of you will picture just " a wee hoose 'mang the heather "—and God forgive us if we are ever ashamed of it. Some will see in vision the old garden— grossets and crab apples; others will recall a village green where they first learned to play the game, and some will envisage that grey city by the northern sea and its open gates under the hoary crown of culture. We feel the scented breath of the bog myrtle as we glimpse the dear homeland—we see the purple moorland, the moorland that nursed us; the rivers and forest which gave us knowledge; we lift our eyes to those Scottish hills, that " iron wall of freedom," under whose rugged majesty we learned the passion of our fathers' liberty and their reverence for the mystery of eternal things. It is not enough to say that Scotland is the Land o' Cakes because the folk there make good oatcakes. It is because the diet of Scotland—simple material diet and spiritual diet; and these make a good blend—has made Scotland what it is. What is the result of that diet ? The three popular charac- teristics of the folk who are nourished upon the oatmeal diet of Scotland are: (1) Piety; (2) Pecuniary masterliness; (3) Power to attain to a place in empire. These are popular fictions based upon permanent facts. The piety fiction is represented by a man in a kilt, a red nose, a toorie to match and an elongated jaw, rebuking his canary because it dared to " whustle " on the first day of the week. Or as we have seen it in the picture of the wee boy chasing a hen round the manse garden with a stick in his hand and shouting, " I'll teach you to lay an egg in the minister's garden on the Sawbath day." That is pure fiction; but what of the fact? Do we not claim something distinctive for the Scottish religion? What is the story of Scotland and the Scottish freedom apart from our religion? Surely the strength of the national life has been found in the sacred influence of our spiritual tradition, which has shaped our history, particularly in times of crisis, as in the Great War, when the religion of the clachan has proved the strength of our people. The real makers of Scotland are those who lived their lives and shouldered their burdens and taught their children to live in the fear of God, performing their task, moved by a spiritual tradition.

The second popular traditional characteristic is our pecuniary masterliness. In fiction we see it illustrated by the two Aberdonians (brothers) who travelled from Stonehaven every day into the granite city. One of the two brothers died, and the body must be taken to Aberdeen for burial. "Very good," said the stationmaster, "but you must buy a ticket for him." "What!" exclaimed the heart-broken brother, "a special ticket for him? The corpse is expired, but his season ticket doesna expire till the end of next month." That again is gross fiction; but what of the fact? The Scot is thrifty in order that he may be generous. And for sheer open-handed generosity who will outrival the Scot? In the capital of the empire, when the churches were asked to contribute to the London hospitals, it was neither St Paul's nor Westminster but the Scots Kirk in Pont Street that eclipsed every other church in the metropolis by £305.

The third characteristic of the Scottish diet is that it produces men who are fitted for distinguished service in the empire. I do not hold that Scotsmen hold every office among the " high heid yins "; there are exceptions! Recently in a Ceylon paper I read something about Home Rule for Scotland. There is, however, one fatal condition which, in my humble opinion, must for ever prevent Home Rule from becoming an accomplished fact in Scotland. Were we to recall from London all the big Scots who are helping to run the empire, in order to care only for the prosperity and happiness of

Bonnie Scotland, what would then become of poor old England ? What of the great Church of England were we to withdraw the two Episcopal leaders in recent years, Canterbury and York, both braw Scots ? What of the English stage if we were to call back men like Forbes Robertson, son of an Aberdeen journalist, and Matheson Lang, son of my father's colleague in the capital of the Highlands ? And what of English education if we were to keep to ourselves in Scotland the Chancellor of Durham University, a Scot ; the Chancellor of Liverpool University, a Scot ; the Chancellor of London University, a Scot ; and the Chancellor of Cambridge University, also a Scot ? No, no ; Home Rule for Scotland would be all right for the Land o' Cakes, but what about the land of roast beef ? Alas and alas !

I would also ask the guests who are not Scots to toast the Land o' Cakes with us, for you, too, have mostly tramped the heather. And so I call upon you, sons and friends of the heatherland, heritors of a great tradition—a toast to Scotland, its hills and dales, its glens of romance, its mist-girt isles, its fir trees and the old peat stack. To Scotland, its two great capitals, classical and commercial—Auld Reekie and St Mungo, Princes Street and " Sauchie," Paisley and Aberdeen, Inverness and the loneliest sheiling in the farthest glen ; to Scotland and its spiritual freedom. I ask you to honour this toast with that unrestrained enthusiasm which is fitting for those who have not forgotten and who to-night pledge our tryst once again for the sake o' auld lang syne.

Many years have passed since I took my last lingering look at the palm-fringed shore of Sunny Ceylon, " Island of Jewels," as the Chinese called it. Sometimes I wonder if ever again I shall see the pond covered with the red lotus ; or watch the colourful sunset to the music of the waves breaking on the Galle Face shore ; or pass under the night of stars along the narrow white road that winds through the fascinating jungle leading to Trinco'. In a land of Come-and-Go, as Ceylon surely is, the friends pass on more swiftly than is the case at home ; but I still retain some happy links for which I am grateful. Unfailingly I receive from the minister of St Andrews the magazine of the kirk; and in it I read a few names of men who were stalwarts in my own time there.

But often it is in the record of deaths that I read with sorrow the passing of old familiar friends. The Dutch Reformed Church, which worked in close harmony with the Church of Scotland, keeps me in touch with their vigorous activities through their monthly *Herald*; and once in a while, from Kandy or the lovely heights of Newara Eliya, a letter comes, refreshing as the crisper air which we used to relish in those higher regions of the Island, where the breath of the breeze was another of God's beautiful gifts.

Politically, and it may be socially, great changes have come over the land of Lanka. The spirit of the age, which was but coming to birth in the years of my residence in Ceylon, has asserted itself; Orientalism has stirred the hearts of the Sinhalese and Nationalism has played an increasing part among their ardent youth, who are too young to know and appreciate all that the colony owes to the British planters, among whom the pioneers were for the most part Scots—the majority from Aberdeen and twelve miles round about. Who else could have faced the task and cleared the jungle : and does not a tour of the estates bear evidence of it, with such names as Hatton, Forres, Banchory ?

The planters in one area are spoken of as the Ratnapura Highlanders. While in the Island I made many friends among all creeds and castes. I was the first Christian minister to be invited to deliver a lecture to the Young Men's Buddhist Association in Colombo under the chairmanship of Dr G. P. Malalasekera, M.A., Ph.D.(Lond.); and a Buddhist priest, after a happy railway journey together to Galle, arranged for one of his temple tutors to give me tuition in the playing of the tom-tom. In recollection of fellowship and ministry in the " Pearl of the Orient " I send my salutation across the seas dividing.

> " Walking here in twilight, O my friends,
> I hear your voices, softened by the distance,
> And pause, and turn to listen, as each sends
> His words of friendship, comfort and assistance."

ABERDEEN AWA'

" There's an old University town
Between the Don and the Dee."

—DR WALTER C. SMITH.

ON my return to Scotland in 1929, with the encouragement
of my former Professor James Cowan, I accepted a call to the
North and Trinity Parish in Aberdeen. At that time the
church, which had been at an earlier period one of the most
flourishing in the city, was at its lowest ebb and several hundred
pounds in debt. Some people thought that it would never rise
again. Trinity Church in Marischal Street was on the eve of
being united with the North Church of St Nicholas when I
undertook the united ministry of the two parishes, with the
assistance of Mr W. Rhind Stuart who was to be succeeded
by the Rev. Robert Macpherson, whose untimely death while
on active service as a Chaplain to H.M. Forces was greatly
lamented by all who knew him. Ministry in that united parish
was a full time job; in fact, for the first two years it was a
continuous overtime; but, with many willing and enthusiastic
workers both within the eldership and without it, the congregation swiftly came to life again and in two years' time,
when we celebrated the centenary of the old North Church,
there were no fewer than twelve organisations for old and
young actively flourishing, the debt had been cleared away
and a manse had been secured. And here I would pay tribute—
my sincere tribute—to the late Mr Alexander Farquhar who,
throughout my ministry, was beadle of the church. He was
appointed on my own recommendation out of over sixty
applicants, and I continued to have increasing satisfaction in
the choice which the kirk session had made. Not blessed
with good health—the result of his active service in the 4th
Gordons in 1914-18—he was nevertheless all that a beadle
could be, and his personal loyalty expressed itself in a final
gesture when, on my departure to my present parish, he
insisted on accompanying me to see me inducted. Pittodrie

had no more staunch supporter than Mr Farquhar, and I recall the occasion when a young couple came to the church vestry one Thursday evening and arranged their wedding for a Saturday afternoon. A disgusted glance from Mr Farquhar flashed it into my mind that the date fixed was the very day and hour of the Aberdeen-Rangers match at Pittodrie, which meant that neither he nor I would witness the struggle. But as the young bridegroom and his betrothed were leaving the vestry I expressed the wish that they would be as successful in their approaching married life as I hoped Aberdeen would be on the Saturday of this wedding. They halted as if struck by a bullet. " Great Scot ! " said the bride-elect, " that's the day of the Rangers' match ! " So back they both came to make some rearrangement, and in a few moments the date was carried forward to the following Saturday. My beadle beamed all over, and as soon as ever the door had closed on the departing lovers he grasped my hand and said, " You handled that business well, Mr MacEchern, but it was a near thing. I'll say it ! "

In 1930 the magic wand of the artist Mr Bennett Mitchell, M.B.E., D.L., effected a welcome and very pleasing trans-formation of the church. In the same year a most successful bazaar, opened by the Marquis of Aberdeen on a day of drifting snow, realised the handsome sum of £550. Then, as the work of the church for myself began to ease off, in great measure due to the rallying round of excellent leaders for the various organisations, I had more opportunity of visiting other parishes in the city and the surrounding countryside on the occasion of their annual socials or as lecturer. At a Deeside soirée I told the following story—with a sequel. A minister was just about to commence his sermon in a country church when his keen eyes observed a young farm lad and an attractive lass talking and tittering in the gallery. Looking up at them from the pulpit he said, " I observe in the gallery a young lad carrying on with a lassie. Now, young man, when you are finished I'll commence." After the soirée I overheard two of the younger members of the congregation bidding each other good night. " Will we be seeing you in the kirk on Sunday, Wullie ? " asked one. And the other replied, " Aye, A'll fairly be there ; and in the gallery too ! "

In the course of my Aberdeen days I had the pleasure of delivering an annual lecture-recital in the ballroom of the Music Hall. I was fortunate in my chairman on those occasions, including Lord Provost Edward Watt, Professor Baird and the Rev. John Ellis, the minister of Rubislaw Parish. Mr Ellis, I always maintained, was the most outstanding preacher in Aberdeen at that time and the Rev. John Ross of Holburn West its most efficient pastor. In my programme a series of tableaux, historical or otherwise, provided a popular item and I was favoured in having as my soloist Miss Violet Davidson, who had commenced her distinguished musical career when, at the age of sixteen, she was appointed leading soprano in the North Parish Church. No one could have entered more whole-heartedly into the spirit of those recitals than she did, and her presence on the programme was mainly responsible for the full house on each occasion. " Those Were the Days," " The Flight of Fashion," " Let Me Introduce You " and " The Humour of Advertising " were among the lecture titles through which the funds of the church were from time to time augmented. In these I was assisted on the platform by the versatility of the Rev. Charles Forster, the Rev. J. Kellas and the Rev. William McNaught.

Although never even approximating to the record number of marriages performed by my father—somewhere in the region of seven thousand—I became very familiar with the Marriage Service. The weddings were not always promiseful of happiness ; sometimes I felt that I was aiding and abetting in a crime ! How well I remember the high-stepping damsel who presented herself in my vestry and gave me the necessary particulars for her impending marriage. " And who," I inquired, " is the happy bridegroom ? " Still admiring herself in the mirror she said in a swift sentence, " Gee, the boob's a real he-man ; hud your tongue—some sheik ! " There was an evening marriage to be celebrated in the church and the hour appointed had struck, when everyone was present except the bridegroom. This suggested some negligence on the part

[*Photo by C. V. A. MacEchern*

ST ANDREW'S SCOTS KIRK, COLOMBO

[*To face page* 56.

of the best man to whom I put the question, " What has happened to the 'groom ? Where is he ? " To this the Albion Street resident answered, " He's oot on the pavement; he's scared stiff to come in ! "

It is the bride's privilege on her greatest day to be late, and I am always indulgent. But once I myself was the delinquent. The marriage had almost escaped my memory and arriving at the church twenty minutes after the appointed time I detected a light in the eye of the bride's mother which clearly suggested battle. But before she had time to open out with her own complaint I proceeded to apologise profusely to her daughter and added, " As a matter of fact I had completely forgotten about this great occasion and very nearly did not come at all." With a gracious smile which greatly comforted me the young lady said, " Dinna worry, minister; I very nearly didna come mysel'."

In connection with the educational lectures given in the Scottish prisons I had the privilege for a number of years of paying an annual visit to Craiginches, Aberdeen, as well as to the prison at Peterhead. On the occasion of my first visit to the former of those institutions the Governor, Mr Wallace, who was the friend of every prisoner, informed me and his uniformed audience that it was my own father in Inverness who was the first to give such a lecture in any Scottish prison; so that, in appearing on the prison platform, I was following in father's footsteps. Possibly my lecture on that occasion was more entertaining than educational; at any rate, on the morning following, Mr Wallace while on his rounds asked one of the female prisoners how she had enjoyed the minister's lecture. " I fairly enjoyed it," she answered. " I know that minister fine. Many a time around his church corner he has got me out of trouble." And then very impressively she added, " That's a godly man, though you wouldn't think so ! " It was a back-handed compliment, but she meant well.

At Peterhead I lectured on " Some Memories." But what made the strongest appeal to most of the audience was my highly coloured delineation of a student escapade in which we had come into mild conflict with the police. Students

5

were students in those days; and after all the police were only doing their duty—that is what they are paid for ! I concluded by inviting any of my audience, when they had more time, to call upon me at the manse in Aberdeen and I would show them the chin-strap of a policeman's helmet, a trophy of the fray. Within two days a gentleman—one of the listeners—called upon me. He had taken me at my word !

No audience is more easy to address than a prison audience. There is a soft spot in every heart. The first essential is to create an atmosphere, and the best way to do so is to crack a pleasant joke at the expense of the warders ! You can then go right ahead and be quite sure of an attentive and interested audience.

In the model lodging house in Princes Street the Presbytery of Aberdeen conducted Sunday services throughout the year under the convenership of my former college friend, the Rev. A. Morrison of Woodside North Parish. These were services which I greatly enjoyed, and I look back with pleasure upon the Armistice Service which I conducted there on several occasions, with the Union Jack draping the table and a vase of red poppies giving a touch of colour to the meeting. I always felt that it was unfortunate that these services were held late in the evening at the end of an exhausting day when the minister was tired ; for they are occasions which demand the very best of the speaker. On my leaving Aberdeen, one of the last friends I met was a distinguished " cat burglar." " I'm afraid I haven't managed to reform you," I said. His answer was : " Don't worry, sir ; you have done me no harm." When visiting such unfortunate members of the community I always kept two scriptural texts in mind. " If my soul were in your soul's stead . . ." and " All souls are Mine, saith the Lord."

In North and Trinity the Boys' Brigade Company, the Girls' Guildry, the Life Boys and the Junior Choir—the last of these under the masterly leadership of Mr John Chalmers—all afforded me a very great amount of pleasure and satisfaction. I continue to maintain that the Brigade and the Guildry are unsurpassed by any other youth organisation for the making of character and the furnishing of the young folk with a healthy outlook and preparation for life. Unlike some other movements, excellent in themselves, they have the church as a background and the Bible Class is an invaluable part of the training; and one of my happiest experiences was the Battalion Camp at Aboyne when I was Chaplain, with the Brigade President, Mr Bennett Mitchell, as O.C. There was a fine blend of discipline and delights, and at night in the great marquee the evening prayers at the end of a perfect day. On widely scattered battle fronts through the years of the Great War many of those same boys must have been glad for the earlier fellowship and training and must have felt themselves stronger in the highest kind of courage in their hour of testing. A Second World War was near at hand when my ministry in Aberdeen came to an end; and on an early morning in March 1938 my wife and I set forth in our car on the two hundred and forty-one mile journey to the parish of Kirkmabreck in Grey Galloway by the Solway shore.

IN A HEBRIDEAN ISLAND

" *If it's thinking in your inner heart the braggart's in my step,
You've never smelt the tangle o' the Isles.*"

—" The Road to the Isles."

FOUR decades have gone since I left the Hebridean Island of Coll and first set foot in the Scottish capital. There, for three days, I steadfastly denied myself the picturesque and novel attractions of the city, for my mind was fixed upon the purpose of my visit—the Preliminary Examination. Confident but nervous I entered the portals of the great examination hall; but the papers set proved to my liking. My brother Dugald, the minister of the parish by the waves, had coached me well and six weeks later the Island postman delivered into my hand the letter which cheered my expectant heart but which sealed my doom, writing *finis* to my happy boyhood on " the edge of the world." The post deliverer was known as Johnnie-the-Post. Post days were the major days of the week, for the

mailboat " Fingal " from Oban called at the inner islands
only on three days of the week on the outward trip.   There
was no wireless in those days and we hungered for news—the
Glasgow Herald with its war telegrams and casualty lists from
the African veldt ; the *Penny Illustrated Paper* with its lurid
pictures of our troops in bloody action ; and the *Oban Times*
with its local items from the pen of our correspondent, Allan
Johnson—the Concert at Acha, the School Prize-giving, the
Wedding of Calum and Kate, and the famous Ploughing Match
at Gallanach which has come down in history.

The postal delivery was equalled in excitement only by the
arrival of the baker's bread from Glasgow, when the
" Hebrides " dropped anchor on Friday afternoon.   Doubtless there are motor vans nowadays, stocked with an infinite
variety of provisions ; but Angus MacFadyen boasted nothing
more than an ordinary farm cart lined with straw, and in
addition to his basketful of loaves his store consisted of jars
of jam—black currant and strawberry, and perhaps marmalade,
Annacker's sausages, tinned tongue, candles, paraffin and
matches.   The stock varied only at the approach of Hallowe'en,
when rosy-skinned apples and nuts found a ready sale at every
door on his sixteen miles circular route.

Angus was well versed in literature and could hold his
own with the student home from college.   The culture of the
Highlands was his possession.   If we sometimes felt that
Angus had missed his vocation, we knew it was not so with
John Kennedy.   Highland postmen are born not made ; and
Johnnie-the-Post was a postman born if ever there was one.
He was short of stature and bulky for his height, and his
cheery countenance and happy greeting were a tonic in themselves.   Parcels and letters in their official bags were packed
into his " machine," which was drawn by the faithful pony
which did duty on the croft on alternate days ; and whatever
the post-office regulations might be, Johnnie could always
find a corner in his vehicle for other deliveries—groceries from
" the shop," which indulged in no message boy ; a tin trunk
belonging to a daughter of the Island who was returning from
service on the mainland ; and a five-gallon cask of paraffin

oil for the manse, where the minister burned the midnight oil and was even reputed to have been met on one occasion by his housekeeper at seven o'clock on a fine spring morning carrying his study lamp still alight to his bedroom, the volume which he had been devouring all night under his arm !

Johnnie-the-Post was the most obliging man in the Island and there was never an afternoon but he picked up two or three of the toddlers from the school at Acha and gave them a " hurl " along the two or three miles to their homes at Ballard or Breachacha. Johnnie would have made a fine referee on the football field, for he was a master of the whistle, with which he announced his arrival at the farms and cottages ; but there was no football in the Island at the period of which I write, save when the Glasgow Fair folk made their annual invasion bringing with them for a certainty the spherical symbol of an advancing civilisation. " There'll no' be much for you to-day," Johnnie would say in his soft Celtic tongue as he sorted the letters. " There's a letter from Sandy in Australia ; that would be taking eight weeks in coming. I hope it has good news for you. And here's a postcard from Jeannie. She says she'll be home for the Fair Week." Johnnie made no secret of his practice of familiarising himself with the contents of the postcards. " Wait a wee ; I'm not sure but there is a parcel for you. Yes, it is from Tobermory, but it is not saying from whom it will be. Now, that's your little lot, so I'll be moving on." " Have you room in your machine for the minister's magic lantern ? " the recipient of the letters asked. " He left it here after his lecture last Friday on ' The Matabele Campaign.' " " Och, I'll find room for it all right ; hand it up. They're telling me it was a grand lecture. The minister should have been a soldier himself." And a soldier he did become ten years later, when the dark cloud blackened Europe and the Great War called the sons of the Island to the defence of the world's great liberties.

Breachacha Castle, a comparatively modern building, stands beside the romantic ruins of the old. How proud the laird, Colonel Stewart, was of his Royal Stewart line, and how charmed to show his guests the room where Dr Samuel

Johnson slept when visiting the Island on his Hebridean tour. But to the boys at the manse, six miles distant, the Castle was most intimately associated with the laird's afternoon TEAS, to which we were invited from time to time. Was there ever Madeira cake like it? And the colonel's eyes would twinkle as he instructed the butler Burgess to " cut that cake as the manse boys like it ! " So we feasted; and then homeward bound with swinging kilts, over the broad uncharted " plain " or, if the mood were on us, through the " sands," where the bent grew high and the seagulls nested, home as the sun was setting.

The sun still sets in a ball of glory over the Western sea; the Atlantic waves are breaking on the rocky shores, sending the spindrift high and far; in spring the plovers cry as of yore, sweeping fiercely down upon any who dare to intrude upon their nesting sanctuary in the low-lying marshy ground; the waters trickle down from Ben Hough, and the burn where we guddled makes music beside the old manse garden; but alas ! the manse is derelict to-day. The old order changes. The laird is gone, the village schoolmaster is gone, and the children of that day are scattered far and wide. For the sons of the Island answered the bugle call forty years ago. Was it not I myself who laid in his soldier's grave Duncan Ross, a son of the Free Church minister, and placed a sprig of heather from the homeland in the wreath which marked his resting place in the Island overseas where that other fighter, the apostle Paul, was shipwrecked while voyaging as a prisoner for Christ's cause. And Hector of the other manse, with a song ever on his lips, true son of his mother in the richness of his generous nature, ready to give always rather than to take. Hector, too, crossed the wide ocean when the bugle called, and he likewise is of the past, because of the shadow and the sorrow that came. But the past, the present and the future are one—parts of a greater whole. The day will break and the shadows will flee away. Johnnie-the-Post has only to blow his whistle over there and the old comrades and friends will forgather.

THE KING GOES PAST

BELLS are tolled and the great guns boom
As the King is borne to his royal tomb.
Streets are thronged with a silent crowd,
Fixed is their gaze, their heads are bowed.
Drums are muffled and pipers play
A haunting lament on this sad day;
And every flag is hung half-mast
As the King on his lone, long way goes past.

Cottars and kings alike must obey
The summons that comes at the end of the day.
" Dust to dust " is the sentence read,
But not of the spirit is it said;
For love and courage and goodness all
Outlive that dust 'neath the purple pall.
Cold in the grave the shell may lie:
God and the soul can never die.

Beyond the range of the human ear
Silver bugles are sounding clear;
Open wide are the gates of gold,
Entries to glories spoken of old.
Confidence stirs in this heart of mine
As Reveille is sounded within the shrine.
So we leave the body beneath the sod,
But the soul of the King goes on to God.

IN GREY GALLOWAY

CROMWELL, according to old tradition, wanted the artist to paint him " wart and all." But a close-up is not the most successful kind of portrait. When one attempts to sketch a parish or district, perspective is needed. So I find myself handicapped, and a true portrayal of Galloway as I see it must be held over until I view it from a greater distance. The years through which I have lived in this corner of Scotland have not been normal years, since they have coincided with the Great War and its immediate aftermath. Coming to the country after seven years in the luxurious city of Colombo and an equal number in the University city of Aberdeen, each with its own special attraction, I have missed some things in my present parish. There is a popular notion that the life of the country minister is an easy business compared with that of the toiling ecclesiastic in the fog and turmoil of the city. But I question whether many ministers who have had experience of both would subscribe to such a claim. Certainly I am not among them. In the work of the city church the leadership is distributed; in the country more is left to the minister himself. There is another idea prevalent: it is sometimes expressed by summer visitors, who imagine that the country people require no holiday, since it is *all* a holiday with them! Standing on the railway station platform setting forth on my summer holiday in the fourth year of the war I was asked, perhaps not altogether seriously, whether my holiday was absolutely necessary. "Most definitely," was my reply. "If I did not take this summer holiday, you could not live with me next winter!" Holidays are essential; they ought to be made compulsory. There was a native from the little Island of Gigha who was induced to pay a visit to his grand-daughter in London. On his return to the village his cronies gathered round to hear his story. "And what did you think of London, Lauchie?" "Och well, London's all very well; but my, my, it's no' like Gigha!" Their sense of comparisons reminds me of the man from an isolated town in the North who took advantage of a special day-trip to London (fare, thirty shillings) to accompany the local shinty club, who had arranged a fixture with the London Scots. Arriving at King's Cross station he sauntered forth and engaged in friendly conversation with the first policeman he met. "You'll be having a busy day in London to-day, policeman," he said. "Oh no; nothing special, nothing out of the ordinary." The Highlander was amazed and said, "Oh yes, you'll be fearfully busy to-day; there's a special trip up from Auchnaleary."

But the country has its own attractions and advantages, and Galloway is not so well known to the tourists as it deserves to be. In the parish of Kirkmabreck there are two seasons which afford particular attraction—the spring-time, when the first green appears upon the larches and the very roadside is coloured with a succession of floral delight. On the twelve miles highroad from Creetown to Gatehouse you travel along a highway bordered by a profusion of primroses and other wild flowers, and if you step into the woods you find the ground carpeted with a haze of hyacinths. For the hill-climber there is Cairnsmore, which dominates the landscape; or if something more in the way of mountaineering is desired, there is the beckoning heights of the Merrick.

The other season is the late autumn, when the entire countryside is ablaze with a radiancy of golden glory and almost every tree aflame with fire. The day is made musical with the song of birds, and for the ornithologist Galloway is a happy hunting ground for his study and delight.

Visitors to Creetown express pleasant surprise to discover on the King George V Playing Fields two all-weather tennis courts, and many find their way to the bowling green where weekly competitions add to the interest of the game. For visitors without cars there is a hiring establishment, enabling them to visit the neighbouring towns and places of interest. These include Newton Stewart—six miles distant, just across the border in Wigtownshire on the winding Cree—and Kirkcudbright, twenty miles along the coast, of which Lord Cockburn in his " Circuit Journeys " wrote: " I doubt if there be a more picturesque country town in Scotland."

Galloway claims to be the area in Scotland to which St Ninian first brought the Christian Gospel. In Whithorn is the old Priory Church over which the late Rev. Harry Law, who was also Clerk to the Presbytery of Wigtown, presided. Possessing a perfect command of the Doric, which he reserved for special occasions, he was equally at home in the pulpit and on the concert platform, and as a raconteur he had few equals. But this part of Scotland is not more kirk greedy than other parts. Wherever in Scotland I have ministered I have discovered that there are but two classes of church-goers: those who are so regular in their attendance that the minister notices at once if they are absent, and those who are so seldom in the pew that the preacher is immediately conscious of their presence on the rare Sundays on which they make an appearance ! In this south-west corner, as in other parts of Scotland, the real hard work in the church is performed by the women of the congregation, and many a minister would find it difficult to balance the church accounts were it not for the income provided by the faithful undertakings of the various branches of the Woman's Guild. Even among the children and youth, it is the girls who rally round the more enthusiastically, as those know best who have undertaken the production of juvenile cantatas or dramatic plays. Among organisations which appear to flourish successfully is the Women's Rural Institute, each branch enlivening the village life with Tattie-peeling Competitions, Grannie Parades, and Kitchen Comedies. The district is dramatically minded and some teams have gone far into the Drama Festival, while the Creetown Silver Band is well known far beyond the borders of the three counties.

Galloway abounds in old historic ruins, some of the castles having been taken over by the Ancient Monuments Department. But even more numerous are the ugly ruins of old houses falling to pieces. The Community Councils might do well to keep their ears open to the criticisms of visitors and do something to remove those unsightly and dangerous derelict buildings which are an eyesore to the æsthetic.

For the antiquarian Galloway affords an interesting field for study and investigation. In Creetown there is no more erudite student than Adam Birrell, whose knowledge of bird life and nature-study makes him a welcome companion for professional zoologists and amateurs alike, and his fine Galloway brogue adds to the fascination of his talks. The staple business in the parish of Kirkmabreck is the quarrying industry, and the Creetown granite is of an equal fame with that of Aberdeen.

The proof of the pudding is the eating of it; and the best evidence of the attractiveness of Galloway is the fact that the same visitors return from year to year; and more would come if accommodation could be found for them. They are given a kindly welcome from a warm-hearted people, and, in my own parish, not less cordial at the Parish Church set upon the hill, whose bell rings out its call to worship forenoon and evening throughout the year. Not far distant stands the

Roman Catholic Chapel—St Joseph's. At a recent entertainment held in the Waverley Hall on behalf of funds for the heating of the chapel, the parish minister sat side by side with the priest who, in his remarks as chairman, declared: " I feel as proud as Punch to have the minister of Kirkmabreck sitting beside me at our show, and with him his flock." In the lesser matters we agree to differ, but in the common task to which we have each been commissioned we enjoy a measure of mutual encouragement; for there is one faith, one baptism, one God and Father over all, our Lord to Whom we all bow the knee. The only other religious organisation in the community is The Brethren, whose meeting place is in Harbour Street. Loyalty to their own tenets does not lessen their ready friendliness to those outside their circle. Unity and uniformity are not synonymous; there are diversities of gifts, there is difference of thought and of method, but we are all one in the greatest of all crusades.

MALTA AFTER THE SECOND WORLD WAR

Proud our salute ! as we approach the Isle
Of epic fame.
Island of Honour—Freedom's iron wall,
In days of old the Bulwark of the Faith
Christ-given to men.

IN the summer of 1946 my wife and I had the happy privilege of spending three months in Malta renewing our acquaintance with old familiar friends in the Island of earlier romance. Malta has a strange fascination and appeal to those who have known it and come under its spell. Its romantic story covers a period of three thousand years, which embrace the six months of the Great Siege in 1565, when Malta proved itself the champion of the Cross against the threat of the Crescent; the years of the First Great War, when it was accorded the title " The Nurse of the Mediterranean "; and the Second World War, when the courage and endurance of its garrison and people won for it the coveted bestowal of the George Cross.

Only when one looks upon the ruins of Valletta can one realise what the Island must have gone through during the years of siege and peril in the Second World War; for all around there is devastation. I had the privilege of studying the personal record of the Rev. Hugh S. Purves, the Scots Naval Chaplain, and from it I learned that of the first hundred Sundays of the siege there were raids during the forenoon service on no fewer than seventy-four. Once there were three alerts between the opening psalm and the benediction; and yet they never missed the Sunday worship throughout the entire period, although on occasions it had to be held in some other building. The part played by the minister and congregation, in recognition of which the former received the O.B.E., is referred to by the Chaplain in these words: " Every family in St Andrew's congregation welcomed the servicemen and women —lonely soldiers from remote country billets and sailors cut off from their families for years—and shared their dwindling rations with them." Malta was a concentrated target—no more than 144 square miles; and between midsummer of 1940 and the end of 1942 over 14,000 tons of bombs were dropped upon it and more than 24,000 buildings were demolished. For our loss of 568 aircraft the enemy sacrificed 1,129. But the Battle of Malta was finally won, and the Empire saluted proudly the R.A.F., the Royal Navy and the Gunners.

Referring to Sir William Dobbie, the Governor of the colony through that anxious period, who was a regular attender at the Scots Kirk service, Mr Purves wrote: " By his moral leadership, his sincerity of mind, his consecrated purpose and his justice above all party and flattery, he won and retained the whole-hearted trust of the simple Maltese people."

On this recent visit to Malta I experienced a measure of disappointment on discovering that so much of the old simplicity had departed, and for that we must lay the blame more upon ourselves than upon the Maltese people. Modernism has already marked their social life; they have to a great extent discarded the national dress worn by the women—the Faldetta—which, I must acknowledge, is not at all suited to the new method of travel in the crowded buses which run to all corners of the Island. Peasants from the country villages who bring their produce for sale in the city can scarcely be recognised as such, and from every second house you hear the blare of the wireless. I missed the soft note of the guitar which was formerly so familiar in the evenings around St Julian's, when gallant troubadours sang to its accompaniment their love songs outside the homes of their beloved; and the quiet walk in the fields or by the water's edge has given place to the wild careering of the motor cyclist with his dark-haired lady seated on the pillion. The priests are strong in their protest against many of the innovations, and during the summer of 1946 the police authorities used the arm of the law to deal with the too daringly attired bathers on the crowded sea-front.

In an Island where the annual rainfall averages no more than eighteen inches, the profusion of wild flowers and garden blooms is astonishing—all richly scented. Lovely blossoming oleanders line some of the roads and giant geraniums climb up and over the walls, and the red poppies in the cornfields provided a study for more than one picture by an Irish Academician. When the first rains fall, almost within the lapse of hours, out of the long parched earth there spring into welcome bloom the lovely jonquils. These were my wife's favourites and greedily she gathered the earliest blooms. It was her passion for these that prompted me to write this little lyric :—

A Jonquil in the Field.

" Come back," said the jonquil in the field,
" When I raised my scented face,
There was none to stoop with a welcome smile ;
Why don't you come apace ?
Come as you came when life was young
In your girlish garb of grace.
When the earth was bare and the pools were dry,
I came with the first spring rain ;
I waited and watched with eager hope,
I waited, alas, in vain.
Had I lived but a day in the cool of your home,
I had not bloomed in vain."

TO HER CROWNING COMES THE QUEEN

2ND JUNE 1953

JUNE cannot boast a fairer flower
Than the Queen who comes to her crowning hour,
Marked by a pageant unsurpassed,
The Flag unfurled on every mast;
Fanfare of silver trumpets loud,
And the loyal welcome of the crowd.

Soldiers of every Regiment,
Veteran lives for their country spent,
Sailors who shared in the great sea fights,
Airmen whose deeds in the lurid nights
Saved our Island from direst fate
And kept our shores inviolate.

Never has London seen such blaze
Of colour and pomp along its ways;
Rulers of every Land and State
Within the ancient Temple wait;
Peers of the Realm their homage pay,
Acclaiming their rightful Queen this day.

There in the Abbey the symbols chaste
Are given, and in her hand is placed
The Holy Book in which we find
The oracles of God enshrined.
The psalm is sung, the prayers are said,
And the Crown is set on her royal head.

Now on her knees she humbly prays
For guidance throughout the coming days,
Trusting in Wisdom from above,
Her heart made strong through an Empire's love;
Ready to write a glorious page:
The new Elizabethan Age.

C. V. A. MACECHERN.

MY BEST STORY

A YOUNG Scottish journalist, on the staff of a well-known weekly, called upon me one evening armed with his notebook and pencil. He had but one question to ask me: What did I consider my best story? I gave it to him as I give it to you. It was one of those occasions when you feel yourself to be an utter fool; when you want the floor to open up beneath you and swallow you up. And to think it should have happened within the historic Palace of Holyroodhouse. The occasion was an afternoon reception during the General Assembly of the Church of Scotland, and on the way to it my wife unfortunately got the point of her parasol into one of her stockings with damaging result. We were in Princes Street at the moment and we dashed into Jenner's to purchase a new pair. A few moments after my wife had disappeared to change into the new stockings the assistant came to the counter with those she had been wearing. There was, however, no time to wrap them up, and I hastily thrust them into the pocket of my long clerical coat. At the Palace, after the formal introductions, Colonel MacRae Gilstrap, aide-de-camp to His Grace the Lord High Commissioner, invited us to have a chat with His Grace and his beautiful lady. It was in the course of relating some experience to the latter that I drew forth what I imagined was my handkerchief and, as I dusted my nose, I saw the eyes of the lady opening wide in astonishment. It was some moments before I realised that, instead of a handkerchief, a lady's long silk stocking was dangling from my hand. Can you imagine my confusion and the apoplectic blush that spread over my cheeks? The lady had not forgotten the incident when I related it to her some years later in Ceylon.

ENVOI

OUR diaries cannot go on for ever. One year will be the last for each of us; one entry will mark the grand finale; we shall lay down the pen and the book will be closed. But another book will be opened.

" And I saw the dead, great and small, stand before God. . . . And another Book was opened which is the Book of Life."

Am I unorthodox or too whimsical when I dare to think that it may be just the Old Diary ?

" And the dead were judged out of those things which were written in the books, according to their works."

Quite recently I was present at the Jubilee Celebration of my University Year at Aberdeen. It was a happy occasion, although the company, after all these years, was not large ; for some of the old comrades are in far places and others were " lost in the storm." But we spent the evening with student song and sentiment, recalling the distant days *consule Planco*.

If my reminiscences in these pages have been largely personal, after all we are far more alike than different ; your experiences have been mine, as mine have been yours. So I dare to hope that what has afforded me pleasure in writing has given you also a measure of pleasure in reading. In rehearsing some of the old deeds, in recalling the friends of other days whose loyalty has stood the test of the years, and voices of the past, the question suggests itself—*Can voices cease ?* The singer may be silent, but surely the song goes on. One at least comes back to me, and how popular it was on the platform at the beginning of the century. It is a song with a message.

> " I shot an arrow into the air,
> It fell to earth, I knew not where.
>
> .   .   .   .   .   .
>
> I breathed a song into the air,
> It fell to earth, I knew not where.
>
> .   .   .   .   .   .
>
> Long, long afterward in an oak,
> I found the arrow, still unbroke.
> And the song, from beginning to end,
> I found again in the heart of a friend."

H. W. LONGFELLOW.